Spheres of Group Analysis

Edited by T. E. Lear

Group-Analytic Society Publications

Second Impression, 1985

Printed by The Leinster Leader Ltd., Naas, Co. Kildare, Ireland

TABLE OF CONTENTS

PREFACE

In this volume I have gathered together accounts from professional people of many disciplines, whose work is widely representative of psychiatric services, social services, higher education, specialised treatment of sexual deviants and problem drinkers, the use of the large group and clergy training.

The contributors write from their practice experience, and it is a tribute to the genius of Dr S. H. Foulkes' teaching that such diverse endeavours could be enriched thereby and to his method that it so beautifully adapts to different demands made on it.

Foulkes inspired the foundation of the Group Analytic Society, the journal "Group Analysis", a thriving group analytic practice and finally the Institute of Group Analysis. The reader will find a good account of the origins and context of group analytic psychotherapy among the psychotherapies, but some may be surprised to learn of the developments of specialised treatments and applications in higher education and professional training.

The Institute of Group Analysis sponsors introductory groupwork courses in Cambridge, London, Manchester, Northampton and Oxford and a higher training course in London leading to qualification for membership of the Institute.

I believe that these British writings will be relevant to course members. Others too, who are interested in groupwork, may draw on this book, which conveys something of the learning from these courses.

Some authors start with practice experience and move towards conceptualizing it, and others, as for instance in the chapters by Dr Malcolm Pines and Dr Pat de Maré, proceed from theoretical considerations towards practice. The reader may be impressed, as I was, that each contributor reveals that the struggle to learn is made worthwhile by new vistas of practice and that each is not satisfied nor prepared to accept that his methods are set in their ways. Like Foulkes he expects group conducting and self-discovery to go hand in hand until the end.

EDITOR

The Origins and Development of Group Analysis

By ELIZABETH T. FOULKES

Introduction

Group analysis or more specifically, group-analytic psychotherapy, is an intensive form of treatment in small groups. The term group analysis also includes applications of the principles both within and outside the therapeutic field. While fully based on psycho-analytic insights it is not an application of psychoanalysis to a group but a method and technique based on the dynamics of the group. It is therapy *in* the group, *of* the group and *by* the group, the group providing the context in which the individual person is treated. Intra-psychic processes are seen as interacting within the mental matrix of the group as a whole.[17]

As a field of study this multi-personal approach aims at finding "a method and theory which would do away with pseudo problems such as biological versus cultural, somatogenic versus psychogenic, individual versus group, reality versus fantasy"[14] and thus searches for concepts that do justice to an integrated view.

"Psychoanalysis . . . has laid great emphasis on the psychogenesis of illness. In group analysis we are more concerned with the outlook for change and the direction and means whereby we ensure it. We therefore work with operational concepts, formulated and applied in the therapeutic process itself and derived from immediate clinical observation."[14] Malcolm Pines, in his contribution to this monograph, discusses the boundaries between psychoanalysis and group analysis.

"Foulkes conceived a new frame of reference for psychotherapy of the small group. He created a new language with which to describe his experience and concepts, much of which has passed into daily use, perhaps without sufficient realization of how these terms originated from the mind and person of a singular individual."[27] It is, therefore, useful to consider the personal development of the originator of group analysis.

S. H. Foulkes was born in Karlsruhe, Germany, in 1898. He died in London in 1976. He received his basic and postgraduate medical training in Heidelberg and Frankfurt, and also spent several years in Vienna for his psychiatric and psychoanalytic studies. His psychoanalyst was Helene Deutsch and Foulkes remained closely identified with the strictly Freudian school of psychoanalysis.

Already in 1919, during his pre-clinical studies in Heidelberg, he read Jaspers, Gruhle, and others on psychopathology and, discovering Freud, knew from then on that he wanted to be a psychoanalyst.[15] He took for granted the need for a thorough training in medicine and neurology. Apart from psychoanalysis, a major influence on Foulkes was the neurobiologist Kurt Goldstein,[21] on whose staff at the Frankfurt Neurological Institute he worked for two years. There he absorbed the holist view, viz. that the whole is more elementary than the parts, which is strongly evident in his group-analytic concepts.[27] Returning to Frankfurt in 1930 Foulkes joined the recently established Frankfurt Psychoanalytic Institute and was appointed the first Director of its clinic. Among his colleagues there were Heinrich Meng, Karl Landauer, Erich Fromm and Frieda Fromm-Reichmann. There was also lively contact with Max Horkheimer and his colleagues at the Institute of Social Research (later to be known as the Frankfurt School[22]) who shared premises with the Psychoanalytic Institute.

Another early stimulation were two papers by the American psychoanalyst, Trigant Burrow. Burrow actually coined the term group analysis but later abandoned it for 'phyloanalysis'.[5/7/8] Foulkes was also much intrigued by plays without heroes or conventional plots such as Maxim Gorky's *The Lower Depth* and Pirandello's *Six Characters in Search of an Author*. Abse has described these sources in some detail.[4]

Early in 1933 Foulkes left Germany and settled in London, obtaining a British medical qualification. While practising as a psychoanalyst he wondered what might happen if his patients, lying on the couch one after the other, could meet, react to and interact with each other. The first chance of putting these ideas into practice came in wartime, at Exeter, in 1940. "I shall never forget the impact which this new experience made upon me. I forged my method and technique through trial and error . . . Ever since that time the theory of the therapeutic process, of change in humans altogether, has remained in the foreground of my thinking. The practice of group-analytic psychotherapy is, as it were, the experimental situation in which theories are continuously put to the test of observation and are reformulated and revised."[15] (See also Foulkes' brief paper reprinted in this volume).

Foulkes' first account of group analysis was written, jointly with an Exeter colleague, Mrs Eve Lewis, in 1942, whilst waiting to join the Royal Army Medical Corps, though it was not published until 1944.[19] He had heard that, in the U.S.A., Paul Schilder and Louis Wender had been experimenting with groups on a psychoanalytic basis but found later that they had been far less radical than his own approach.

At Northfield Military Hospital Foulkes practised group therapy on an increasingly large scale and contributed to the creation there of the first 'therapeutic community' when group methods were used throughout the hospital.[13/25/26] After the war Foulkes and a number of colleagues founded the Group-Analytic Society (London) to further the theory and practice of group analysis. Foulkes had an appointment at St Bartholomew's Hospital and from 1950 he was consultant psychotherapist to the Bethlem Royal and Maudsley Hospitals. Other members of the Society had appointments at St George's Hospital, St Bartholomew's, the Cassel and other hospitals in the London area.

Foulkes called the method group analysis or, more specifically, group-analytic psychotherapy. The special emphasis of the method he defined early in a triple sense;

(1) active participation on the part of the members
(2) communication
(3) observation in a social setting[13]

It is *not* psychoanalysis in groups, unlike other methods of group psychotherapy practised by psychoanalysts. From the first Foulkes emphasized the group situation; all events and statements are considered in the context of this particular situation. The group-as-a-whole is seen as a *gestalt,* the emphasis being frequently on the total group or part of the group, with the psychopathology of the individuals as a background; conversely the attention may be focussed on one member, or the inter-action between two members, against the background of the group context. (Another strand in Foulkes' theoretical formation was his contact with the Gestalt School of Psychology in Frankfurt). The interest in the group session is focussed on the 'here and now', i.e., on what is happening in the group as it is meeting. The 'there and then' of individual group members is fully accepted as it comes up spontaneously through 'group association' but it is not particularly searched out. In fact, if patients go back again and again to early childhood events and feelings, as they would in the two-person psychoanalytic treatment situation, this is considered a defensive manoeuvre.

The group itself is the medium of therapy and the group-analyst pays special attention to the interactions of members with each other including transference relationships, laterally, to each other, to the group-as-a-whole as well as to himself as an authority figure. This position of the group conductor as the expert, expected to 'cure' the members, is one which will be slowly relinquished. Foulkes speaks of a *decrescendo* movement on the part of the therapist as the central figure, balanced by a *crescendo* move towards integration and self-reliance on the part of the group.[14] In the course of time, and also with the growing experience of any particular group-analyst, it has become evident just how much may be left to the group itself. Group members are highly sensitive to each others' problems and feelings. They listen to and accept probing questions and criticisms readily from their fellow patients.

The conductor (called thus rather than leader, since he does not generally lead the group) is responsible for selecting and matching the group members. Under out-patient conditions they are usually a heterogeneous group, matched less in regard to psychiatric labels but more to avoid isolates by too great a span in age, intelligence and educational background; usually half women and half men. In these stranger groups members should have no relationship with each other in real life. Foulkes preferred the term 'proxy' groups to stranger groups to underline the transference element in the interaction.

The number of members may be between five and ten, the preferred number being eight. Groups of out-patients usually meet either once or twice each week, the sessions being for one and a half hours at a regular time and place.

The group sits in a circle, with the therapist or co-therapists, preferably on identical chairs rather than on a makeshift assortment. Otherwise the group-analytic situation is relatively unstructured. There is no programme or topic for discussion, nor are activities such as psychodrama or painting introduced. The importance of such matters as regularity of attendance, punctuality and abstaining from social contacts outside the group sessions is brought to the group's attention as being desirable in the interest of their treatment, rather than being presented as 'rules'.[16]

The action remains on the verbal level. What develops is a 'free-floating discussion', often turning into genuine 'group association'. Members will try to re-establish relationships within the group in a familiar mould, which can be seen in terms of repetition-compulsion, repeating long-established patterns of behaviour; de Maré has suggested the term 'transposition' rather than transference for these relationships.[9] Unlike some group psychotherapists who emphasize the group as representing for each member his family of origin[28] group analysts consider this as only one particular aspect of varying interactions on different levels which are observed dynamically in the group process. The concepts of this process are not taken over directly from the dyadic psychoanalytic situation but are always seen as arising from the group situation. Among 'group-specific' therapeutic factors which have been described is for instance: 'mirror-reaction': this does not merely imply seeing oneself or part of oneself mirrored in another person, but is a multi-level concept encompassing the psychoanalytic concepts of projection and identification.[6/19]

'Translation' from the inarticulate symptom to verbal expression is the group equivalent of making the unconscious conscious in psychoanalysis. The group provides a setting for action, reaction and interaction. This has been described as 'ego training in action' i.e. the ego (in the psychoanalytic sense) is amenable to activation and change.[14]

Communication, the vehicle and instrument of group analysis, takes place on many levels, all of which are observed by the group conductor who lets his attention silently float from one wavelength to another, as it were. The current level is where the members consciously share their experiences and feelings; the transference level often represents their families of origin; on the projective level other members personify part of the self; the 'primordial' level corresponds to the collective unconscious of Jung.[14] Though observing these different levels the group conductor does not automatically confront the group with the links which he may have found. He is, in fact, sparing with interventions and interpretations and carefully considers their timing.

The process by which a patient's symptoms can be translated and communicated in terms of conscious mental conflict is a long and difficult one. "... both psychoanalysis and group analysis are intended to be basic, radical, central therapies but ... the areas in which they each make their main attack differs. The group-analytic situation, the horizontal analysis, sheds more light on the immediate present, on the here-and-now and on the immediate life situation of the patient. It concentrates more on the analysis of this immediate situation and has more direct effect upon it. It reveals less of the patient's individual genetic development and the origins of his disturbance."[18] "Social and cultural factors determine the individual's inner structure decisively. Syndromes, diseases, their very existence and the form they take cannot be understood outside their sociocultural context ... The study of small groups, in particular of an analytic kind, has proved a good instrument for practice and research in this social field."[20]

Considering the individual's own personal network in his current life, Foulkes writes: "In the group-analytic view the processes operate and interact in the total psychodynamic field of the network group, its matrix passing, as it were, right through the individuals of this group . . . Hence I prefer to speak not merely of interactional processes between individuals, but of transpersonal processes."[20]

"Illness and related disturbances are due to psychopathological processes which thus involve a number of interrelated persons. The individual can be seen as a participant in a drama. In the psychoneuroses this *multipersonal network of interaction* is of central significance. Change in any one member of such a network is linked to change in other members of this network. I have been impressed increasingly over the years by observations which seem to show that even the nature of an individual's symptoms or other manifestations of tension rest on this interdependence. This group of interrelated persons, e.g. the family group, should always be considered as the framework for diagnosis and prognosis, even where a simultaneous approach to the whole group is not practicable.

"Illness emerges as a social, interpersonal process. Its psychosocial analysis is of particular value in bringing to light the concealed meaning and significance of the many guises in which illness appears."[20]

The application of group analysis to the natural group such as intimately connected networks has developed side by side with stranger groups. The family is the prototype of such groups, although friends, colleagues or neighbours may well be involved. "The great importance of such an approach lies in the theoretical consequences it has for our view of psychopathology and of the social nature of mental processes . . ."[16] Robin Skynner has attempted the integration of a group-analytic and a systems approach in his rich and valuable book on family therapy.[29]

Harold Behr's contribution to this monograph will be dealing with the group analytic approach to family treatment.

Wider applications of group analytic concepts to groups of all kinds are manifold, e.g. in education, sport and industry. 'Learning, that is vital learning, presupposes a change of attitude concerning the whole person. If used in this sense there appears to be no clear cut difference between the learning and the therapeutic processes.'[23] Jane Abercrombie's work in applying group analytic principles in higher education is outstanding and well documented, and her contribution to the present monograph is essential reading.[1/2] She has also written a fascinating paper entitled 'Foulkes and Escher; Visual Analogues of Some Aspects of Group Analysis.'[3] She employs the multi-perceptual levels in the work of the Dutch artist M.C. Escher[11] to illustrate the group analytic situation.

A relatively more recent development is group analysis applied to median (20-30 members) and large groups (up to 120).

Groups of twenty to thirty persons have been convened now for several years by P.B. de Maré and have proved to be of great interest. 'The small group by its very nature displays only the most fragmentary evidence of social dynamics. To apply small group or psychoanalytic models to the large group is like trying to play ludo on a chess board. The large group, on the other hand, offers a context and a possible tool for exploring the interface between the polarized and split areas of psychotherapy and sociotherapy.' And later 'While the problem for the members of the small group is how to feel spontaneously, for the large group it is primarily how to think.'[10]

Groups of one hundred persons and more are regularly held as part of the Introductory Courses of the Institute of Group Analysis in London, replacing the weekly lectures and demonstrations for one term. Robin Skynner comments 'As with all large groups, the situation is too complex for one person to grasp, and the emotional pressures so great that multiple leadership is an advantage; this is especially valuable if it is truly multiple, with room for normal expression of disagreement among the leaders.' 'The impossibility of containing and controlling fully the large group's interaction is perhaps one of its greatest assets. We seem each year to be brought to face the most fundamental questions of man's existence, and find emerging themes which illuminate the great myths, legends and religious symbols in new and unexpected ways.'[30]

Pat de Maré's chapter in this volume will throw further light on these exciting developments.

Organization

A small number of colleagues had met informally after World War II to exchange experiences and decided in 1952 to found the Group-Analytic Society (London). The first weekly seminars were given by Dr Foulkes in 1951/2 since when the Society has been holding regular scientific meetings and has arranged a variety of workshops, local, European and International. Systematic training, including a qualifying course leading to membership, has been the responsibility of the Institute of Group Analysis since 1971.

Annual workshops in London and regular European Symposia offer a forum to colleagues, both from Britain and those residing overseas, for exchange and further experience. There are well-established links with various overseas centres including Australia, Canada, Mexico and the U.S.A. Training courses in group analysis are currently held, in collaboration with the Institute of Group Analysis in London, in Denmark, France, Germany, Greece, Italy, Spain and Switzerland.

The Journal 'Group analysis' was founded in 1967 by S.H. Foulkes and edited by him until 1975. It is a publication of the Group-Analytic Society (London) and is noted for its informal and lively correspondence and commentary sections.

References

1. Abercrombie, M.L.J. The Anatomy of Judgment. London, Hutchinson 1960. Penguin Books, 1969.
2. Abercrombie, M.L.J., Aims and Techniques of Group Teaching. London. Soc. for Research in Higher Education, 1970. (4th ed. 1979).
3. Abercrombie, M.L.J., Foulkes & Escher: Visual Analogues of Some Aspects of Group Analysis. Group Analysis, Vol. 2 146-149.
4. Abse, D.W., Clinical Notes on Group Analytic Psychotherapy, Bristol. John Wright, University of Virginia Press '74.
5. Abse, D.W., Trigant Burrow and the Inauguration of Group Analysis in the U.S.A. Group Analysis 12, 218-229, 1979.
6. Brown, D. and Pedder, J., Introduction to Psychotherapy. London. Tavistock 1979.
7. Burrow, T., The Group Method of Analysis. Psychoanal. Review, 14, 268-280, 1927. (German Translation: Die Gruppenmethode in der Psychoanalyse. Imago 12, 211-22, 1926).
8. Burrow, T., A Search for Man's Sanity. Selected Letters of Trigant Burrow. W.E. Galt *et al* (eds) New York, Oxford Univ. Press 1958.
9. de Maré, P.B., Perspectives in Group Psychotherapy. London Allen & Unwin 1972.
10. de Maré, P.B., The Politics of Large Groups. In: Kreeger, L. (ed) The Large Group, London. Constable 1975, Maresfield Reprints 1984.
11. Escher, M.C., The Graphic Work of M.C. Escher. London; Oldbourne. 1961 2nd ed. 1967.
12. Foulkes, E.T., Notes on the early days of the Group Analytic Society (London) Group analysis 10, 104-108, 1977.
13. Foulkes, S.H., Introduction to Group-Analytic Psychotherapy, London. Heinemann, 1948. New York. Grune & Stratton 1949.
14. Foulkes, S.H., Therapeutic Group Analysis. London. Allen & Unwin 1964: New York, International Univ. Press 1965.
15. Foulkes, S.H., Some autobiographical notes. Group analysis 1, 117-122: 202-205, 1968.
16. Foulkes, S.H., Group-Analytic Psychotherapy: Method and Principles. London & New York, Gordon & Breach 1975.
17. Foulkes, S.H., The group as matrix of the individual's mental life. In: Group Therapy 1973, Wolberg, L.R. and Schwartz, E.K. (eds) New York, Intercontinental Medical Book Corp. 1973.
18. Foulkes, S.H. and Anthony, E.J., Group Psychotherapy, the psychoanalytic approach: Harmondsworth, Penguin Books 1957 (3rd ed. 1973).
19. Foulkes, S.H. and Lewis, E., Group Analysis. Brit. J. Med. Psychol. 20, 175-184, 1944. (reprinted in shortened form in Therapeutic Group Analysis 1964).
20. Foulkes, S.H. and Prince, G.S., (eds) Psychiatry in a Changing Society, London. Tavistock 1969.
21. Goldstein, K., The Organism: A holistic approach to biology derived from pathological data in man. New York, American Book Co. 1939.
22. Jay, M., The Dialectical Imagination: a history of the Frankfurt School and the Institute of Social Research 1923-50. London, Heinemann 1973.
23. Kadis, A.L., Krasner, J.D., Winick, C. and Foulkes, S.H. Practicum of Group Psychotherapy. New York, Harper & Row 1963.

24. KREEGER, L. (ed) The Large Group: dynamics and therapy. London, Constable 1975, Maresfield Reprints 1984.
25. MAIN, T.F., The Hospital as a Therapeutic Institution. Bull Menninger Clinic 10, 66-70 1946.
26. MAIN, T.F., Contribution to a special scientific meeting of the Group Analytic Society (London) in honour of the 70th birthday of Dr S.H. Foulkes. Group analysis 2, 133-137, 1969.
27. PINES, M., The Contributions of S.H. Foulkes to Group Analytic Psychotherapy. In: Group Therapy 1978, Wolberg, L.R., Aronson, M.L. and Wolberg, A.R. (eds) New York Stratton Intercontinental Medical Book Corp. 1978.
28. SCHINDLER, W., Family pattern in group formation and therapy. Int. J. Group Psychother 1, 100-105, 1951.
29. SKYNNER, A.C.R., Systems of Family and Marital Psychotherapy, New York. Brunner/Mazel 1976. (British edition entitled One Flesh: Separate Persons. London, Constable 1976).
30. SKYNNER, A.C.R., The Large Group in Training. In Kreeger, L. (ed) The Large Group. London. Constable 1975, Maresfield Reprints 1984.

A Short Outline of the Therapeutic Processes in Group-Analytic Psychotherapy

By S. H. FOULKES
(January, 1975)

In group-analytic psychotherapy we look on all mental processes as interacting in the group-as-a-whole. The individual's disturbance – neurotic in the widest and fullest sense of the term, or even physical – is considered only as a symptom within the context of his group. The disturbed individual is a symptom of a disturbed group. The most simple and elementary example of such a group is the family. When the family is disturbed, it has a negative effect on the change or improvement in any one of its members. It is only fair to add that the family supports its members while its equilibrium is good, and helps them to function and to balance their weaknesses and disturbances.

The nuclear family imbues and impregnates the individual, from his earliest phase of life and even before birth, with the total value system of the culture of which this family is a part. In addition, each and every relationship within this family must be seen as reflecting the particular and specific family culture which is prevailing.

The simple model is that of the nuclear family of parents and children. If they can be treated together, this is a good example of the group being the object of treatment as a whole. Such treatment can be very successful, even if confined to a fairly limited number of treatment sessions. The reason is that the working through can and does take place in the course of daily family life and all members have to change at the same time.

The adult patient whom we usually see under out-patient conditions in hospital or private practice presents himself as an individual. He is naturally also a member of an intimate group with whom his disturbance is interconnected. This current group may indeed include the family but most probably also includes a number of people in intimate inter-action with the patient, his friends, companions, colleagues and rivals. This whole complex of people may be approached as a whole; this does not mean that they all have to attend together at any one time. The result of such treatment can be very good, but it is often not possible in view of practical considerations, and even more because of insuperable intrinsic opposition arising from conflicting interests. Nevertheless having made this contact and seen the interacting plexus in operation is still a step of considerable psychodiagnostic and prognostic value. It shows very clearly how far this particular patient can change within his present context of living or is more or less prevented from so doing. Such a patient is better treated as an individual, either in the two-person situation or in a group-analytic group where he meets strangers with whom he has no other contact in life. When we thus focus on the individual patient we again look at him as a whole person in the first place.

The holist view in my own case links up particularly with my apprenticeship with my teacher Kurt Goldstein who did pioneering work in that direction. Our patients were physically brain-injured people, as the result of wounds received in the first world war. What Goldstein could demonstrate was that the organism always reacts as a whole, that the central nervous system is an interconnected network which reacts as a whole. Localised defects did not cause, as was thought, limited effects in specific functions. The resulting clinical picture represented rather the response of the whole nervous system, the whole organism, to the defect inflicted on it. Disturbed function could be demonstrated in all spheres; the whole world in which these people lived was characteristically changed. The lesion naturally coloured the total picture more or less, according to its localization.

In a certain sense, Goldstein's orientation was in sympathy and fitted in with Gestalt theory. We worked together with Gestalt psychologists and I thus learned more of their theoretical holist approach than I otherwise would have done. The insight that the whole is more and earlier than the summary of its parts belongs here. One can understand the parts from the whole, but cannot build up the whole from the parts.

The possibility of seeing the processes in a group on the basis of figure-ground-relationship can also be seen in this context. For instance, one can focus on an individual or individuals as the foreground with the group as background; or vice versa, on the group-as-a-whole as foreground, as figure, and see the individuals' reactions as ground. This becomes important both theoretically and practically when we have to deal with the relationship of the individual to the group, or vice versa. I believe that these two can never fully be separated and that many of the problems of their relationship are therefore pseudo problems. I believe that it is most useful to put the processes of *com-*

munication and the commonly held ground, the *communion*, into the centre of one's consideration, which processes comprise at one and the same time the total field of group and individual together.

The difficulties which arise from these insights from the point of view of a Freudian psychoanalyst are a separate matter which took me several years to put into perspective and to integrate. In group analysis, as I understand it, there is no such contradiction.

The group-analytic group *sensu strictiori* is thus the direct opposite of the natural or life group. It is impossible to neglect either individual or group and, as I express myself, the individuals have to be seen and treated in the framework and context of the group of which they are members.

The individual who joins this group-analytic group – a group of strangers – defends himself by all the means at his disposal against change, as do most of us, especially the more neurotic. He is therefore forced to try to re-establish as far as possible the network in which he was originally shaped and in which he can function as he is. In this endeavour he is confronted straight away by the fact that he gets quite different responses from the ones he was used to from the other participants in the group. Each individual has the tendency or even the compulsion to turn the group as far as possible into a family, into his family, to make it familiar, so that he can be at home with a minimum of change. It is therefore of the greatest importance that we consider this repetition of the family situation as a cardinal and basic resistance and resolve it through continuous analysis and confrontation.

The group analyst who accepts this pseudo family, and himself merely as a transference figure in it, plays the game of the neurosis and does not bring about its dissolution. It is of course clear that this tendency to re-establish the original family situation in the treatment group is related to what we recognize in individual psychoanalysis and psychotherapy as transference and repetition compulsion. If the therapist himself does not fall into the trap of accepting this family scheme as the basis of his operations the group-analytic group itself enforces decisive changes in experience and of behaviour in the individual member and brings his defences and reaction formations to the fore. The group analyst has a lot to do in helping the hard-pressed ego of the patient in its struggle for liberation, to help it to face new situations and experiences and reactions; to shed old, engrained, but now unnecessary defence mechanisms; to assist in the constant revision and reformation of super-ego demands which take place in the group and which correspond to change in the actual super-ego, the unconscious conscience of each patient. We are here on ground which corresponds quite particularly to the unconscious aspects of ego and super-ego.

Every group has certain positive, supportive and constructive aspects which act therapeutically. The relief experienced by the common sharing and understanding, by exchange and mirror reactions, by the feeling of belonging, by overcoming the sense of isolation and replacing it by socialization should be mentioned here.

Our main concern is about increased, better and enriched communication. Communication is very much in the centre of all processes, therapeutic or otherwise. In its highest form, in its most articulate form, communication is of course verbal communication. Language itself is a good example of what is meant by communication, embracing individual and group at the same time. Each individual speaks his own language, and has to learn it afresh and on the basis of an inherited capacity laid down in his brain. But he learns the language which is spoken around him, at first by his mother and father, and this becomes his language, and yet this language itself is a shared property of the total community. It is not a summary mosaic of individual efforts at communication.

In the group-analytic group everything is taken as a communication, whether it is an incident happening inside or outside the group, so long as it reaches our knowledge and influences what is going on. It is astonishing if one takes this view how many events which seem at first sight to have nothing to do with what is going on are in fact very clearly and profoundly connected with it on further examination.

I believe that a good deal of what is usually called external or social is at the same time deeply internal and of very powerful dynamic influence for the total being as he develops. This comprises our social, cultural, vertical inheritances transmitted over generations, even for the building up of one's own image of one's body, as Paul Schilder in particular has shown. There are some basic things shared by our groups even before the individual members have met, such as language, the particular culture, even class and education. This is called the *Foundation Matrix*. They bring this common ground with them into the group. What we traditionally look upon as the innermost self, the intrapsychic as against the external world is thus not only shareable, but is in fact already shared. This becomes more and more understood in this particular kind of group as time goes on.

We should therefore not really speak of communication *as a process* but as a communion, an existing communal network. Apart from this fundamentally shared life we can see this matrix growing and developing more and more, embracing more and more complex issues which are very important for the therapeutic process altogether. This, which develops under our own eyes, is called the *Dynamic Matrix*. All mental processes, including of course all therapeutic ones, take place in this hypothetical web of communication or communion, in this matrix. If we can accept this view we can imagine mental processes as penetrating the individuals which compose the group – going through them, transgressing them and linking up with each other. While the individual is exposed to these processes he also has a certain modifying influence upon them. There is a constant give and take going on. There is usually a shared zone in the key of regressive levels concerning impulses, defences and the individuals' resonance. Splitting, as for instance into "good" and "bad" objects, manifests itself by personification and polarization. On the primitive levels of this shared psychic reality processes of introjective and projective identification operate among others. They can, however, always be seen to be mutual, or even multipersonal, in nature.

I speak in this sense of the processes as not merely interpersonal but *transpersonal,* suprapersonal in a sense. They are transpersonal processes interacting one with the other according to the laws of psychodynamics. This total process going on inside the shared matrix of the group is the dynamic mother soil in which change operates.

Analytic activity, of which the group itself is the main active instrument under the guidance of the analytic conductor, should be seen as in the service of the group's communication. This is the more so as improved communication in this deep psychological sense at the same time leads to improved and richer and freer communication in each individual. In other words it is in the service of the progress from symptoms to problem and the problem's possible solution.

Our overall aim is naturally change, but in the direction of the increased liberty of the individual which enables him to find himself no longer to the same extent dependent on or hampered by the group in which he inevitably exists. That part of the analytic process that one may call the translation, the helping to make more and more articulate what is being less consciously communicated and shown (though necessary for uncovering and decoding) is less in the foreground of our own contribution than is the analysis of the unconscious ego and superego. As I have indicated these are constantly in action and in interaction in such a group and therefore the conductor's work is different from that of the psychoanalyst in the two personal situation. The conductor is not so much concerned with interpretation but with the uncovering of the unconscious part in the here and now of the therapeutic situation. We analyze the ego in action. We analyze the individual in the group in actual on-going behaviour and reaction.

The most powerful factor in bringing about change and the possibility for further and future progress after the group has ended is based on the ego training in action and not so much on the insight and interpretation based on words as such, as upon the ongoing corrective interaction with others. This is the main spring of the mutative experience in group-analytic psychotherapy.

(First published in Group Analysis 8: 69-63, 1975.)

NOTE: For a full bibliography of the writings of S.H. Foulkes see The Evolution of Group Analysis (ed M. Pines), London, Routledge and Kegan Paul, 1983; also Group Therapy 1978 (eds L.R. Wolberg, M.L. Aronson and A.R. Wolberg), New York, Stratton Intercontinental Medical Book Corp. 1978.

The Frame of Reference of Group-Analytic Psychotherapy

By M. PINES

A full half century after Freud's original discoveries, we have begun to put psychoanalytic technique and the psychoanaltyic situation itself into perspective and to see the framework of psychoanalysis, to see that it has a frame. One of the first to describe this was Marion Milner[24] who wrote "The frame marks off a different kind of reality that is within it and that which is without it; it also marks off a special kind of reality of a psychoanalytical situation, and in psychoanalysis it is the existence of this frame which makes possible a full development of that kind of creative illusion which we called the transference. It is by means of this illusion that a better kind of adaptation to the world ultimately develops". Masud Khan,[18] building on the work of the anthropologist Pouillon, clairfied that what Freud had done was to isolate the patient from his social frame, where his position as a patient was determined by society's frame of reference, and had placed him into a therapeutic frame, into the analytic situation where "the analyst and the patient were phenomena unknown to each other, with no tradition of reliable shared symbols that could help them to negotiate with each other . . . In this new frame the alienated individual could find his symbolic and therapeutic speech and form of expression." Almost half a century later this therapeutic framé was enlarged and no longer one isolated alienated individual but a number of such persons were taken into the therapeutic framework to create a therapeutic society. "Group treatment is the resolve to take a larger part of the external world and of the persons associated into a field of direct observation than is the case of individual treatment. They can now face their problems as a group, including their reactions towards each other. One could say, too, that group treatment means supplying "common sense, the sense of community to a problem by letting those openly participate in its attempted solution who are in fact involved in it". So wrote S.H. Foulkes.[11]

The emergence of analytic group psychotherapy as a theory and as a technique was facilitated by a new scientific paradigm, that of the move from the study of single entity, the item, the individual, to the study of the relationship between an entity and the field of forces in which other entities are encountered. Just as we study particles within the atom, so we look at persons in relation, and the processes that differentiate, link and unite us and which brings us into conflict. We look at social space, and the space between us and the invisible psychological forces that determine the relationship between persons. We are still seeking a suitable model for this; the classic psychoanalytic model of the mental apparatus will not do as it is based upon a one body psychology.[25]

In group psychotherapy we need other models; perhaps a systems model will do,[7] one in which we see how the input of information into a system counters the loss of differentiation and the inevitable run down of the system. This is a model of negative entropy and was not available to Freud as it derived from the much later findings of information theory. As a physicist and philosopher of science, Ernest Hutton[16] wrote:

"In the natural sciences we have reached a point where it is no longer possible to treat the individual for the whole group of them; the system has become the 'carrier' of the action. The stage of classical physics where an isolated piece of matter, the mass point, is the representative of a natural phenomenon, has been passed. With the conventional type of energy transmission, or causality, as the basic relation linking points in space, time or events, has been greatly changed. (For me) to treat the group of individuals which are connected by numerous strong and complex interactions – not an isolated individual acted upon by a single force – provides the motive both for a psychological group theory as well as for a physical systems theory." Hutton also says "Meaning rules human action, whereas cause determines physical processes. The rules of meaning rather than the laws of nature explain human behaviour."[7] Biological systems differ from physical systems and the differences are in the diverse behaviour of energy and entropy, of causality and information of order and organisation. Gregory Bateson has put it very simply; when you kick a stone it moves; that's energy. When you kick a dog it bites; that's information.

Moving to the clinical situation a useful perspective on *the differentiation between individual and group psychotherapy* can be made by looking at the significant variables in each situation. In psychoanalysis it is the phenomenon of the transference; by contrast in a small group it is "relationship"; and in the large group it is "context". This has been pointed out by de Maré.[6] The psychoanalytic situation is carefully constructed and has an invisible yet powerful framework in which transference is aroused and manifested. The techniques for this are the privacy, the use of the couch, free association, the unseen analyst, the fixed time and unchanging space which creates the boundaries of the space time framework of psychoanalysis. This is not simply technique; it is a powerful social situation with its own dynamics, as Trigant Burrow[1/4] was the first to show. He made the crucial experiment of reversing roles with a patient and discovered that the analyst in his new role was by no means immune from the same social forces as had affected his patient. When a patient steps over a threshold into the consulting room he leaves his own social frame and enters into the therapeutic frame of psychoanalysis which was described by Bleger[3] as an "institution".

Bleger says that "a relationship which lasts for years and in which a set of norms and attitudes is kept up is indeed an institution". This unseen, unconscious psychoanalytic frame represents an unconscious primitive symbiosis of infant and mother, part of the undifferentiated primitive early mother/child matrix.

The group is another institution, a "temporary institution",[27] one in which the evolution of norms, values, goals and the institutional factors are much more evident than in psychoanalysis. In the group they are foreground whereas in the psychoanalytic situation they are background. In a group these institutional factors of norms, values and goals become negotiable, for they are constructed out of the potentiality of the group situation. The situation of the group now becomes a negotiable changeable context. The group evolves a culture; the relationships which develop are the medium through which the work of therapy is carried out. It is through the exploration of relationships that changes occur, through relationships that are altered and developed, which can be explored and analysed. The essential group analytic factors of mirroring, that is of discovering part of oneself in the other and being for the other an object of projection, the mutual exploration within the force field and face to face situation of the group; these factors are the crucial ones in the group, they are group specific.[11]

In a small group the power of transference has to be recognized in order to be overcome and has to be overcome before the members can enter more fully into the group situation and take part in and contribute to the network of communication and of relationships through which these change processes occur. By contrast, in psychoanalysis, the relationship context is held constant and this allows transference to come to the fore through externalization of the person's inner world and this renders it accessible to interpretation and change. By contrast to psychoalanysis the group is a "movable, changeable context"[6] of relationships and it is on that relationship context that the patient is compelled to impose his transference pattern which represents the activation of his inner object world and of the dynamic processes which are involved in the creation of these relationships. In a group this pattern is activated, manifested, recognized and then can be altered. Those parts of the relationship, of patterns which eventually will interfere with group development, with the movement of the group towards a more mature form of institution, are not accepted nor confirmed. The other group members who become enmeshed in the transference web will assert their own reality, their own needs. There is a constant pressure to move towards a more healthy balance of relationships and thus the constructive aspects of personality are reinforced and the repetitive and immature aspects are not ultimately accepted.

Of course we have to appreciate the significance of numbers in the difference between the diadic and the group psychotherapy situations. It is not sufficient, however, to bring an arithmetical approach to this difference. The group situation is that of people sitting together, including the therapist, in a face to face situation, in a circle. The group situation encompasses both physical and psychological space and the circle is a space bounded by members of the group. All members of the group, including the therapist, share the same space, the powerful universal symbol of the circle, and I do not think we have yet fully appreciated the psychic significance of that fact – the circle as a symbol of unity. Compare this spatial situation with the "linear" situation of psychoanalysis – with the patient on the couch, the analyst sitting behind unseen, and where communication occurs through the patient's solitary free associations which are responded to sparingly, for the most part, by the therapist's considered words, whereas the group consists of responding persons, reacting to each other in a shared situation. But to return to arithmetic as James Home[15] has pointed out, in psychoanalysis the analyst sees one patient at a time five times a week for an hour. The patient is alone, a singleton. In group analysis the same analyst sees a patient once weekly together with several others for say one and a half hours. "Frequency of attendance in the one situation is substituted by a multiplicity of persons in the other."[15] This again is a simple fundamental difference to which insufficient attention has been paid so far. We know that this treatment situation of a multiplicity of persons with infrequency of attendance has considerable therapeutic power and leverage and that the powers are to some extent those of society, of social psychology. If we contrast the basic dynamics of the diadic situation and those of the group situation, might it not be that the basic underlying dynamic of individual psychotherapy – that is, the patient's fantasy of possession, of refusion with the primary maternal object, and the defences against that refusion — is basically what is worked through in psychoanalysis. The basic dynamic in a group must be different. There is not the same frequency of attendance nor the same intense personal relationship with the only other one present, the analyst. The group members belong together in a way that the therapist does not. They experience themselves as an entity and the basic underlying fantasy that has to be dealt with is that of differentiation, where the therapist becomes an authority figure, rather than the primal mother figure. The therapist becomes seen as the authority figure who can give or withhold cure, a collective group fantasy which has to be worked through. The primary constant dynamic in the group therefore is the individual's relationship to authority whereas by contrast the underlying basic transference dynamic in diadic therapy is that of possession and identity.[15]

I now consider some other aspects of group process that can be viewed from the perspective of *social psychology* and of psychoanalysis, to see if those viewpoints can be integrated.

In social psychology the meaning of an act is understood in its social context. "The behaviour of an individual can be understood only in terms of the behaviour of the whole social group of which he is a member, for it is the larger group that provides the context for individual acts." Thus wrote George Herbert Mead,[23] the American social philosopher, founder of the school of symbolic interaction. Mead pointed out that although any human act can be analysed as the unit of individual behaviour, the content of such an act is typically social because the reflected judgments of others are woven into the initiation and execution of such an act. "It is not just that the other people are present around us that makes their act social; what is more important are the people who are present within us. Other people are present within through symbolic representation."[26]

Mead had shown the self develops in the context of human interaction and that we respond to ourselves as objects of our own subjectivity. As we become selfaware the "I" discovers the "me". Mead showed that the "me" aspects of self comes about through the internalization of the general attitudes of significant others, that we come to see ourselves through the images that have been reflected back to us through the attitudes and actions of the persons with whom we interact throughout childhood. This work follows in the tradition of William James, the looking glass self of Cooley and this approach has had a considerable influence on interpersonal psychoanalysis, the Sullivan approach. But within more orthodox psychoanalysis there has been increasingly emphasis upon the significance of self psychology, self theory and mirroring. In America the work of Ericson,[8] Hartmann,[14] Jacobson,[17]

Loewald,[22] George Klein,[19] Lichtenstein[21] and others have been opening up that approach; the significance of narcissism and the importance of mirroring has been pointed out by Kohut[20] and the Chicago School. For all these writers, self emerges from the undifferentiated mother-child matrix, as it did for Fairbairn,[9] Balint,[2] Winnicott[28] and Guntrip.[13] The undifferentiated matrix of the mother-child unit gives way to the differentiation of infant and mother within the matrix of the entire family. Foulkes, the founder of the Group Analytic School used the term matrix[11] from the beginning of his work to describe the underlying network of communications in the small psychotherapy group. In fact from the group analytic viewpoint it is through the creation of this powerful matrix that individuals can change, can redefine themselves.

Murray Cox,[5] writing of the group as a situation of redefinition and using the theories of group analysis and of Mead, says "if the group is the milieu in which the original process takes place, then ipso facto the group would also be the milieu in which redefinition occurs". This redefinition takes place through the sustained tension of oscillation between the experienced "here and now" of the group in terms of the "there and then" of each individual member of it. "One of the factors which induces changes in the conception of self is that the patient has to some extent a shared here-and-now experience as a member of the group whereas his there-and-then was idiosyncratic and personal. His self-perception influenced by others' perception of him is not as fixed and fossilized as he thought it was. Within the confines of the group, movement occurs as attitudes begin to melt and the possibility of change of self image and behaviour emerge. The patient's ideas of his own identity, his self definition and his definition of others will be constantly challenged and modified. The group process provides not only one mirror but a series of mirrors whose many faceted reflections help establish an individual's sense of his own identity by delineating its similarities and differences in relationship to other members of the group. On reflection, in both senses of the word, an individual is helped to explore what he is not, and therefore among other things "what he is".

I would like to look at this explanatory mode of redefinition using the intrapsychic language of psychoanalysis and in particular the work of Hans Loewald. Writing on internalization Loewald[22] shows how psychic structure, take for example the superego, is formed by the dissolution of previous structures. In this case the superego emerges out of the relationship to the parents during the Oedipal phase. These structural elements of relationships are, as it were, dissolved, assimilated, and in a sense metabolised. There is what Loewald called "a destruction of relationships and structures into their elements. An internal restructuring of these elements occurs within a different *organizational setting* so that novel, but in some ways related, elements evolve". Those internalization processes create and increase the coherent organization and integration of the psyche as a whole. The psyche grows through processes of internalization which start at birth and it is in this way that the infant psyche becomes organized from the undifferentiated mother-child matrix. The child begins to approximate to the stage of differentiation that the mother was in when the interaction between them started at birth.

Loewald contrasted the processes of internalization and of repression. Repression, a defence, works against this process of psychic growth. Freud in "The Ego and the Id"[12] stated that repression represents "an antithesis between the coherent ego and the repressed. "Thus what is repressed is not simply dynamically and topographically unconscious but it is set apart from the "coherent ego". Through repression psychic processes remain in a less organized and more primitive state. By contrast internalization is also an unconscious process but what is internalized becomes part of the coherent ego, in contrast to what is repressed, which is set apart from it. I see an analogy between the higher levels of functioning of a therapeutic group and the action of this coherent ego of the individual which represents his more mature capacities. Those capacities have been attained through on-going processes of internalization and metabolization of previously existing and less highly developed psychic structures. We can see the same process in the group; the norms, values and attitudes of the therapy group can be more mature, more coherent than those of the individual members and the task of the therapist in relationship to his group is mainly to preserve and to facilitate this process. The process was seen by Foulkes[10] as being a basic law of group dynamics.

"The deepest reasons why patients can reinforce each others normal reactions and bear down and correct each others neurotic reactions is that collectively they constitute the very norm from which individually they deviate. The community of which they are a miniature edition itself determines what is normal, socially acceptable behaviour. Each individual is, to a large extent, a part of the group to which he belongs. This collective aspect permeates him all through to his core. As the group proceeds so the individuals find more and more common ground and less and less contradictions between individuality and community."[25]

Each group member is partly isolated from the higher levels of functioning of the group by neurotic patterns, by symptoms which sooner or later will appear as disturbances in types and levels of communication within the network of the group. Working through these disturbances which represent the transformation of symptoms into communication blocks, enables the person, now more integrated, to take a fuller part in the transactions of the group. That, I suggest, is part of the process of individual change in a group situation. It is the move from isolation, which is akin to repression, and it enables him to become part of the coherent whole of the group. That is analogous to the repressed contents of the individual mind now forming part of the coherent ego of that same person.

In a group this process can lead to renewed internalization, when by taking a fuller part in the group transactions the individual is becoming more open to the feelings, responses, attitudes and values of his fellows. This allows new internalizations to take place which in turn now form the aliment for new psychic structures. New identifications can take place between the individual members and between the members and what the group as a whole represents for them, basically maternal and paternal imago. Through these identifications the boundaries of self and object representations become more permeable. There is a merging of self and object followed by a redifferentiation of self and object, each now recognizing their unique identity through recognizing the differences between them. Identification thus is followed by differentiation. Those processes occur because internalization has begun again and each member can now function on a new and higher level of psychic organization. In psychoanalytic language object cathexis is transformed into the narcissistic cathexis that establishes and maintains psychic structure.

Group psychotherapy has to grow and to maintain its own frame of reference. Burrow[4] and Foulkes[10] showed us the way. The growth of our own theories will continue, fertilized by the workers in the neighbouring field of psychoanalysis. Those of us who work in both fields can help by bringing ideas together in the hope of stimulating discussions and a new perspective.

(First published in the International Journal of Group Psychotherapy 31, (3) July 1981).

References

1. Abse, W. (1979), Trigant Burrow and the inauguration of group analysis in the U.S.A. *Group Anal.*, 12:218-229.
2. Balint, M. (1965), *Primary Love and Psychoanalytic Technique*. London: Tavistock.
3. Bleger, J. (1967), Psychoanalysis of the psychoanalytic frame. *Int. J. Psychoanal.*, 48:511-519.
4. Burrow, T. (1927), *The Social Basis of Consciousness*. London: Kegan Paul.
5. Cox, M. (1973), Group psychotherapy as a redefining process. *Int. J. Group Psychother.*, 23:465-473.
6. de Maré, P. (1977), Group analytic principles in natural and stranger groups. *Group Anal.*, 10:16-21.

7. DURKIN, H. (1981), Some contributions of general systems theory to psychoanalytic group psychotherapy. In: *The Evolution of Group Analysis*, ed. M. Pines. London: Routledge Kegan Paul.
8. ERIKSON, E. (1956), The problem of ego identity, J. Am. Psychoanal. Assoc., 4:56-121.
9. FAIRBAIRN, W.R.D. (1952), Psychoanalytic Studies of the Personality. London: Tavistock.
10. FOULKES, S.H. (1948), *Introduction to Group-Analytic Psychotherapy*. London: Heinemann.
11. ——(1964), *Therapeutic Group Analysis*. London: George Allen & Unwin.
12. FREUD, S. (1923), The ego and the id. *Standard Edition*, 19:17. London: Hogarth Press, 1961.
13. GUNTRIP, H. (1971), Psychoanalytic Theory to Therapy of the Self. London: Hogarth Press.
14. HARTMAN, H. (1958), Ego Psychology and the Problem of Adaptation. New York: International Universities Press.
15. HOME, H.J. (1981), The effect of numbers on the basic transference pattern in group analysis. In: *The Evolution of Group Analysis*, ed. M. Pines. London: Routledge Kegan Paul.
16. HUTTON, E. (1981), Meaning and information in group process. In: *The Evolution of Group Analysis*, ed. M. Pines. London: Routledge Kegan Paul.
17. JACOBSON, E. (1964), *The Self and the Object World*. New York: International Universities Press.
18. KHAN, M. (1972), On Freud's provision of the therapeutic frame. In: *Psychoanalytic Study of Society*, vol. 5, eds. W. Munsterberger and A. Esman. New York: International Universities Press.
19. KLEIN, G.S. (1976), *Psychoanalytic Theory*. New York: International Universities Press.
20. KOHUT, H. (1971), *The Analysis of the Self*. London: Hogarth Press.
21. LICHTENSTEIN, H. (1977), *The Dilemma of Human Identity*. New York: Aronson.
22. LOEWALD, H. (1973), On internalization. *Int. J. Psychoanal.*, 54:9-17.
23. MEAD, G.H. (1968), The genesis of the self. In: *The Self in Social Interaction*, eds. C. Gordon and K. Gergen. New York: Wiley, pp. 51-59.
24. MILNER, M. (1952), Aspects of symbolism in comprehension of the not-self. *Int. J. Psychoanal.*, 33:181-195.
25. RICKMAN, J. (1951), Number and the human sciences. In: *Selected Contributions to Psychoanalysis*, ed. W. C. M. Scott. London: Hogarth Press and Institute of Psychoanalysis, 1957, pp. 218-223.
26. SCHELLENBERG, J.A. (1978), *Masters of Social Psychology*. New York: Oxford University Press.
27. SINGER, D., Astrachan, B. Gould, L., and Klein, E. (1975), Boundary management in psychological work with groups. *J. Appl. Behav. Sci.*, 11:137-176.
28. WINNICOTT, D.W. (1965), *The Maturational Process and the facilitating Environment*. London: Hogarth Press.

Reflections on the Experience of Group-Analytic Psychotherapy

By MARIE STRIDE

The pace of change in a nuclear society is such that individuals may easily lose touch with their origins. Subsequently a series of poor adaptations to new situations may leave them in a milieu where common terrors bind individuals together more frequently than common joys. Carl Jung with his notion of the self-regulating psyche wrote that individuals strive towards wholeness of being. There are other ways to wholeness than those offered via psychotherapy or religion. Many people find peace within themselves and ease in the company of others without consciously experiencing either of these mediums. Mental health is more than the absence of disease; the presence of an individual in a therapy group, whatever the model, may indicate he is already seeking a positive component in life, perhaps evaluating his own philosophy or questioning previous interpretations of experience.

Contiguous processes of autonomy and socialization complement each other. Early learning tasks include the acquisition of social skills and the formation of habits that enable individuals to remain harmoniously in contact with each other. Man is gregarious by nature, human experience is shared experience. Through attempting to communicate with others individuals are able to explore and develop their own talents. Separation from others is either an accidental or artificially contrived state, for we need the diversity of others to affirm the unique individuality of ourselves.

Initially identity is built on the reflection we receive from our mothers or caretakers. A conditional or negative response leads to anticipation of conditional or negative responses in daily encounters. Inter-personal transactions with other individuals grow into our intra-personal perception of the relationships we have with them, and are permanently internalized for better or worse.

Predictability is the essence of security and understanding. Being part of a stable well balanced family gives the child predictability, social standards and the beginnings of an internalized capacity to control the self. These attributes enable the child to accept areas of experience without reality testing them. Fire burns, wasps sting, later he will have to unlearn that "jersey is something you put on when your mother feels cold!", but for the vulnerable years he receives the support he needs to allow psychic growth to occur unhindered.

Parents are natural shock absorbers, through their presence the child learns to cope with his emotions. The mother kissing the bruised child is diluting hurt by acknowledging it, not altering the state of physical pain. Within moments the child may experience his mother's pleasure with his being, her irritation with his slowness. Variables in family response expose him to the reality that total harmony exists for indeterminate periods. He learns to accept the vagaries and ambivalences of relationships and becomes familiar with the amalgam of free-floating feelings in constant use, so that the transition from one to another is neither undermining nor overwhelmingly threatening.

One of the stabilizing factors protecting the child in early experience is a network of open relationships, starting with the immediate family, spreading to extended family and community. The network keeps open multiple channels of communication and experience for the child, so that gradually he acquires a sense of alternative identities as brother, cousin, nephew, grandchild or friend. If there is an unstable or interrupted relationship with the caretaker, there is the possibility of the child focussing on a surrogate caretaker from the extended family. Experiences of birth in the community are balanced by deaths. Such events give confidence in the reality of someone having gone before him and the probability of someone coming after him. Exposed to emotional events his coping style will be modelled on that of the adults nearest to him.

The open family system is not only an important safety network for individuals, it also enables them to experience and develop an understanding of intimacy and distance. Relatives in frequent contact with the child may receive a quicker or warmer response than those met infrequently. The child begins to discriminate between distances and responses from the immediate family, extended family or community. He learns to negotiate the varying encounters and adjusts his expectations and response to past experience of the actuality of the situation. It is this development of awareness and understanding of closeness and distance that the child later uses as a base on which to build and differentiate between the public and private self.

The optimal distance for the management of relationships comes easily to many people, for others it remains a continuous struggle to find and maintain.

Away from the natural habitat of the family, humans construct psychic barriers to yield to individual needs yet maintain a positive edge to self. Unidentified needs unconsciously find their own source of satisfaction.

The boundaries between individual knowledge and cultural knowledge are difficult to separate; apparently personal boundaries have a common denominator with culture for they encompass elements of customs and philosophies of the family or social group. Barriers are negative resistance erected to maintain and defend a private space between self and others in which contraction and expansion can occur without the intrusion of others spotlighting every tremor of growth or searching for seismic faults or defects.

Personal growth requires periods of privacy, for over-exposure fades self-image as surely as under-exposure neglects it. The distance between the public self and the private self is intimacy. Isolated moments of inclusion which characterize meaningful interaction occur by transcendence of barriers not penetration of boundaries. Penetration of boundaries is a unilateral action, transcendence of barriers a mutual one. Since barriers are established to aid separation from the family, it follows that by incorporating information from other sources the individual can help modify his own family system by an input of fresh notions, thereby keeping the system open and viable. A child continually deprived of privacy is denied the observation and rest periods essential for integrated development. When early experiences are too fierce and unpalatable he may manage them by swallowing them whole and undigested. He may achieve the necessary privacy by distancing himself from the experience acting as if it was happening to someone else, splitting off and concealing what he believes to be his true self. Alternatively he may cope with that which cannot be coped with by performing some mechanical ritualistic act designed to concentrate mental activity, thereby diverting his emotions from the experience until all that remains is a blurred sense of something unpleasant having taken place in the past.

The absence-presence rhythm of bonding patterns creates cyclical time concepts in infancy, these help establish anticipation as an alternative to rage, hope as an alternative to despair, for as the caretaker (mother or good object) returns to restore the boundaries of self, the sleeping-waking, hunger-fullness cycle is completed. It follows that disturbance of primary bonding processes disrupts stabilization of time cycles. The child unable to provoke a satisfactory response to need, remains in a state of rage rather than risk the nebulous area of despair brought about by unreflected existence, alternatively he may descend deep into despair becoming unreachable.

When contact is restored he may neither tolerate the comfort which precedes future loss, nor is he able to reject the object for he fears the disintegration of self which accompanies separation.

Natural circadian rhythms governed the life of primitive man. As civilization became more sophisticated he was compelled to acknowledge artificially structured clock time. Acceptance of chronological time balanced with the individual's variable psycho-physical time stabilizes a time-bound self. Fusion of linear and cyclical time enables one to accept that the present exists also in the past where it has been shunted for future reference; while the here and now moves forward in chronological time, it still exists in recollection. Once experience descends into recollection it becomes an amalgam with other memories and cannot be extracted without other bits of experience with it. An individual lacking a time bound self fails to recognize today as yesterday's tomorrow and becomes locked in a complex of panoramic memory, unable to relate past events to present situations – every experience is a new experience. Exposed to a continuously revolving landscape of experience juxtaposed without linear or cyclical order, the welter of unstructured images creates a processing problem. Unable to classify or compartmentalize, a montage of events is built up by precisely overlaying them one upon another without selective procedures which might permit superfluous materials to be discarded.

Because he is unable to organize the vast input of information it is difficult for the individual lacking a time-bound self to isolate single items from his dense mass of interwoven data, and it becomes increasingly difficult for him to maintain a coherent thought sequence because he is uncertain which information is relevant to the current communication. Self preservation blocks his receiving ability and turns him into a transmitter only. When this point is reached the individual may deal with communication by the insertion of an action filter, this is a sub-conscious video-recording of events which enables him to take "time out", holding the information in storage for action replay without the accompanying emotions. Such a screening system postpones psycho-physical involvement in communication to the point where it can be tolerated without loss of personal control, thus avoiding a sense of distintegration of the self. The time-space lapse between events and interpretation of their contents permits the individual to operate his retrieval system away from the real or fantasied pressures of other people.

In so far as the individual is able to retrieve information this defence system differs in degree to that of the child resorting to splitting off experience. While the action-filter gives an immediate respite from too intense experience, it also diminishes the quality of the human encounter so that it becomes unrewarding for all involved. In ordinary circumstances the discomforts of too intense experience is usually diluted by the presence of rationalizing others, but such discomforts can be magnified by group collusion.

Linear and cyclical time establish a structure by fixing things into sections of a continuum. Initially this is necessary to maintain direction and give shape and order to what might otherwise be described as intolerable chaos. However, the encapsulation of events in chronological time may freeze them and create a cult of defensive aggression in some individuals, because subsequent experience is received and processed without analysis of currently contributing factors. A repetitive reflex response may lead to polarization of cultures and lay waste opportunities for mutual exchange. Such grossly distorted views may be symptomatic of atrophied relationships where total loss of contact causes individuals to respond to outdated stereotypes rather than to real persons. If images are distilled concentration of memory, then the constant response may be to a stereo-typed bad image. Such a view is dependent on selective perception where vast areas or reality are ignored or denied. This may be a way of denying loss, the rationale being that if objects are bad then there is nothing worth having, nothing lost, nothing to mourn. In denying loss in these instances the seeds of self-destructive behaviour or insidious disease may be sown. When individuals off-load their disillusionment or pain in this way, or where they avoid facing themselves by projecting their own aggressive or negative elements into others, they are not only left with a sense of incompleteness but are inextricably bound to their scapegoat, for they need him to restore the wholeness of self.

One of the most difficult areas of mourning to work through is the loss of a relationship where people are alive and in constant contact. The diminishment of capacities due to accident, illness or senility or their enhancement by natural maturing processes brings about personality changes. As a result of these changes individuals become alienated from each other, or from their group and psychic bereavement occurs which is not always recognized.

An individual locked in unstructured time may become so saturated with the wash of apparently unrelated events that he is forced to extricate himself from the mesh of panoramic memory which permanently records experiences without processing them. Like everyone else the individual possesses the same need to make sense of his experience, by concentrating on the sheer density of material he intuitively penetrates the depths with minimal surface distrubance extracting a core sample of stratified elements. As layers of memories are peeled away there is a reclustering of surface images and a reorganization of information which alters perspectives. Once self imposed pressures for conventional organization of input are lifted, a natural transformation of personality organization becomes a possibility. It is as if he is released from the need of a systematic historical context and is permitted to retain his own valid geographical features in time and space. The reawakening of hope and the vision of growth confirm the finite nature of existence, yet paradoxically reflect infinite possibilities for self awareness, self healing, self creation. Unresolved aggression activated by recall of events in chronological order become modified and is capable of being transformed into positive components extending receptively towards life rather than curtailing it. Such concepts as self awareness, self healing, self creation can be glimpsed but never fully achieved for as one approaches them the horizon enlarges, the sky shifts and one struggles to comprehend the unfathomable grounds of totality.

However good the early parenting, most humans accumulate a number of unresolved experiences which they are unable to discard, since they may at some time help make sense of incomprehensible information. It is possible to live an outwardly successful life concealing a 'slush' fund of unresolved emotional experiences one would like to dispense with and a "trust fund" of good experiences one would like to recover. The emotions that attend unresolved conflicts can lead individuals into negotiating life by avoiding commitment to others. Teaching, preaching, nursing and other 'care' professions carry the possibility of such involvement without commitment. Although they satisfy the need to be needed and constructively use love in universal settings, the practitioners can feel depersonalized and lacking mutuality in relationships, they become increasingly frustrated. The professional himself remains not only alone but is often uncared for. Aloneness is not the need for company but the need for 'kind'.

The meaning of deprivation is the deprivation of meanings. An individual deprived of the language of any social group remains isolated and unprotected without guides to steer him through processes of using and capitalizing on feelings. He has no notion how to absorb, reflect, react to or reject emotional input. Just as his thinking and behaviour may appear to be bizarre and eccentric to others, his perceptions of others may lead to confused bewilderment for they appear to think and behave in ways totally alien to those he knows from integrated areas of early family experience. The mismatch between family and social mores may build up a psychic immunity to the external world and its information systems. When it is impossible to resolve atrophied relationships or develop satisfactory new ones, group analytic psychotherapy offers a "false" family which helps reactivate the unresolved tensions and conflicts which are the stumbling blocks to psychic maturing. With a process of re-education or rehabilitation through personal relationships, these tensions and conflicts can be melted or surmounted enabling the individual to come to terms with the imperfections and inadequacies in all human relationships.

Before some individuals may be comfortably accommodated in a group a preparatory period of individual therapy may be required to neutralize antigens and negotiate areas of expectations and difficulties. There needs to be an acceptance of the individual's differences by the group. Individuals must recognize within themselves areas of similarity with others even if initially it is no more than being fellow members of the human race. Individuals must not feel threatened by demands to conform to mores they do not know or understand, and they need to learn that the group functions as an entity not as a collection of individuals, which may be how they first perceive it. Failure in group therapy, as well as failure in diadic therapy, is likely to cause a retrenchment by the individual into old defences depriving him of a vital opportunity to regulate the undigested conflicts which burden him and impede his development.

Normal human response is to resist uncertainty, discomfort and pain, and all these experiences may be part of an analytic psychotherapy group because such feelings accompany change. Structuring group meetings at regular intervals within a fixed chronological time span, in a specific place provides the security and predictability needed by group members. The time limit of each meeting provides a necessary element of tension needed to keep the group functioning as a growth medium where members change and mature; it is this tension which prevents the meeting degenerating into cosy social occasions where mutual support happens but very little occurs that will spur movement towards personal growth. While individual therapy exposes contributing factors to personal disease, group analytic psychotherapy by its provision of a variety of alternative views of the effect of the disease, offers a greater opportunity for modifying fixed attitudes, demonstrating the truth that we construct our notions on partial impressions.

Language is a cultural phenomenon, a random mix of individuals would produce a new culture but not necessarily a healing one. For this reason psychological grafting on the group to facilitate easier interpersonal relationships needs to be undertaken with care. Participating members in a group analytic psychotherapy group develop their own language and grow their own unique culture free of the indoctrination and conditioning of family, caretakers or external community. As the series of meetings progress a common core of shared history develops. This core not only enables individuals to relate to each other in chronological time, it also gives a learning experience of working harmoniously in the shared history, contributed to by all, satisfying the need for "kind" and permits the gradual suspension of formal constraints so that transcendence of barriers can begin to take place. As old information is re-cycled individuals are able to examine their present reception and response to interactions stripped of past pain or future hope. This is necessary for just as past pain can intensify defences future hope can anaesthetise the self against the painful reality of the present moment. The effectively functioning group provides a safe situation where unconscious intuitive material of individuals can be brought into conscious awareness so that they are able to explore unresolved conflicts and release the stifled emotions that accompany them. By freeing oneself from the unconscious content of mind it loses its compulsive element and leaves one open to alternative ideas. The multiplicity of group notions provides a valuable source of material to fill the vacuum left when one is finally able to discard obsolete views.

One of the early learning tasks of the group is to help individuals separate the "here and now" experience from the "then and there" experience. "He who does not remember the past is condemned to relive it" said Santayana. While one may exclude memory, dispense with articles pertaining to it or avoid situations and people associated with it, it is impossible to dispose of the memory itself. Conversely one may try to manufacture memories by gulping life, acquiring material possessions attempting to plug the gaps of past deprivations, but such acts cannot compensate or satisfy the unattended, unsupported or abandoned child that remains within.

Memory is individual and unique whilst archetypes are common and universal. Through mingling information in a group, memories can be mellowed by committing them to an archetypal pool commonality, or by translating archetypal images into unique personal representations, the preciousness of memories may be recognized, often for the first time.

New understandings grow from living the experience of the group because the conditioned response acquired by experience in the formative years is resonated by the group members. This multiple screening causes one to examine the structure and content of the interaction and enables modification of behaviour to take place as a result of re-interpretation of old information. The task between the meetings is one of diligent reflection, since it is reflection on experience that ultimately leads to decisions and actions. It is reflection which leads individuals from the group into different social contexts no longer feeling isolated or unrelated outcasts as was the fate of the creative dissident in Plato's Republic.

"So if we are visited in our state by someone who has the skill to transform himself into all sorts of characters and represent all sorts of things, and if he wants to show off himself and his poems to us, we shall treat him with all the reverence due to a priest and giver of rare pleasure, but shall tell him that he and his kind have no place in our city, being forbidden by our code, and send him elsewhere after annointing him with Myrrh and crowning him." (part 3, Par 398. The Republic).

The reality of the therapeutic setting is that by exposing needs it is unable to satisfy, it returns individuals to the ambivalent uncertainty or isolation of childhood or traumatic experience, but this time round with the possibility of coming to terms with those needs through the supporting presence and awareness of other group members. Group analytic psychotherapy is concerned with promoting maturity. Maturation depends not on analysis and interpretation but on individuals finding the courage to risk admitting to themselves that they care about the group and need affirmation by its members without calculating or rejecting return dividends from their investment in it. When the individual cares more about the group than he does about himself, his need is such that he will modify his own behaviour in order to remain harmoniously in contact with them.

It is the individual who learns to be "totally present" in the group, not the ones who are passing on the way to somewhere else, who become most vulnerable to change, for it is a simple truth that the more that goes out from one the more room remains inside one to absorb new ideas, new experiences. It is this "being present" in the group that opens one to the unscrambling of tortuous resistances. Personal change in the individual precedes the acquisition of insights which mellow rigid attitudes by uncovering the possibility that while one may have previously stored correct information one has not necessarily processed satisfactory understandings of life experiences.

In the microcosmic reality of the group one gains confidence to test and accept realities of race, culture, class, creed, sex, physical impairment or temperamental idiosyncracies. These cannot be changed, but it is possible to modify attitudes towards them. While ethnic origin remains unchanged self regard for one's primary culture can be grown. Sex or achievements previously under-rated in the search for perfection or alternatives can be valued for their own merits. The misguided self which formerly tried to deal with separation and loss by splitting off or deferring memory thereby causing further separation and loss, gains courage to recover and re-integrate memories, for as Shakespeare worte in Sonnet 116:

> "But if the while I think of thee, dear friend,
> All losses are restored and sorrows end".

Finally, there is an awakening to the truth that all those things which harm or destroy the self arise within the self, for we grow our own worlds and carry them with us always. As one gets nearer to the crowd the less it appears as a solid threatening mass, rather the crowd becomes a loosely arranged bunch of people with whom one can communicate on many levels. In opening oneself to others one becomes a fragment of the crowd and is healed by it. The affirmed self is no longer narcissistically preoccupied but is able to utilize energy and resources for enjoyment and involvement with the world and its people.

Unswerving truth and rigid integrity are the course of saints or sickness; there must be some sort of credibility about human performance if individuals are to remain intact and in contact.

Credibility lies in striving for perfection while acknowledging that the humanness of one's condition makes missing and failing at times inevitable. It also lies in retaining the courage to continue striving towards goals once set if they remain appropriate, or in abandoning those goals if the flux of daily existence and personal development renders them inappropriate. By modifying and transforming self-annihilating behaviour, self alienated parts of one's being can be re-integrated making wholeness a possibility. When this happens one becomes capable of a constant re-defining of the new self at the expense of the old, thus by a process of reconciliation living becomes gaining not losing.

Perhaps a summary of the outlines of the principles of Group Analytic Psychotherapy is best set out in the prayer:

> "O Lord give us the serenity to accept the things we cannot change,
> The courage to change the things we can and
> the wisdom to know the difference."

The Experience of Group-Analytic Training

By T. E. LEAR

The Institute of Group Analysis (London) has a *General Course* in Group Work which is held annually and consists of thirty half day sessions, held over three terms. The events consist of lecture/discussion sessions, an experiential small group and a large group. This is introductory as far as those who go on for the Qualifying Course are concerned. Treatment, theory and supervision make up the tripos of training in each course. I shall describe my experience of the *Qualifying Course* under these headings.

Treatment

At an interview with a psychiatrist at the Institute of Group Analysis I found that I was recounting my professional experience and triumphs with ease but a scenario in my past I described slowly and sparsely. The details in the scenario no doubt had personal significance, but the difference in how I dealt with external and internal matters was noticed and reluctantly acknowledged. I was reflective and I had understanding about myself but this was by means of thought and half thoughts, not systematically entrusted to spoken words. I realized that to have personal insights was one state but to share them with others another.

The Institute training policy was to have a trainee placed in a twice weekly treatment group comprised of both trainees and patients conducted by a senior group analyst. I was pleased but felt this to be painful submission as well. Resistances associated with unresolved authority issues were well in play as I accepted the offer of a place in his group at an interview with the group conductor. I couldn't pretend that this was simply training when I hadn't been accepted yet on the qualifying courses. On the other hand, once in the group the trainees could regard themselves as therapists rather than patients and the patients could deny that they could participate in any way as therapists and we could collude thus with a mutual denial of the possibilities of exploring certain experiences. Here the payment principle entered into consideration for it dawned on me that I would be paying to provide treatment for others and not for myself. This would be going beyond the Foulkes principle. Foulkes' idea in group analytic psychotherapy was that group members would come to participate with the conductor in the analysis of the group or of the individual in the group. I remained in this group for four and a half years and since it was a slow open group people joined and left at a slow pace. I oscillated between fears of changing my ways of seeing and those of being unable to change.

I was confounded by excessive pretensions to bring about change in all directions and trussed by my own rigid control. I strived to impose on others in the group the roles and reactions of family members past and present, but those others wouldn't have it. Their objections, questions or puzzlement baffled me for I was hearing something unfamiliar. Though this was not my family, yet I had space to roam and move between boyhood and manhood freely. I had time enough to pause and reflect. I could be playful and laugh, moved both in ways I could understand and which were inexplicable. I was confused and felt impotent at times and yet I felt the support of others in the group. The past was brought to the present for each member bit by bit and during those years many and varied life experiences were brought to the group but the group had a life of its own as well. Members joining and leaving, absences, lateness, subgroupings and encounters outside the group were illuminating for each of us by their analysis. Not only could individual members be seen to change in how they interacted in the group as well as by their reported inner and social experience but the group as a whole lurched unpredictably from cohesive to dissonant atmosphere and communications became gradually of a quality to allow for sensitive, intimate exchanges between members, or a member and the conductor. My preoccupation with the conductor in the early stages of treatment became modified so that I was aware of the potential of other members as well. The pain of envy of him and others I gradually acknowledged until it became a bit more bearable and in consequence I experienced the advantages of sensible sharing with others in the group.

An assessment panel appointed by the Institute Training Committee interviewed me. The panel had a report from the psychiatrist who interviewed and one from my group conductor. A recommendation from the panel Institute Training Committee resulted in my acceptance on the Qualifying Course. A group of Course members, all graduates from various professions including general psychiatry, child psychiatry, psychology, music therapy, psychoanalysis, social work and psychiatric nursing, were together in various seminars over several years. Some of those people were likely to share the same supervision group but were less likely to be in the same treatment group.

Theory

The psychoanalytic schools and concepts, the development of group work in treatment and training, the small group, large group, residential therapeutic community and natural group such as the family, were studied in detail from psychological, sociological and systems theory viewpoints. Dr Foulkes' presence and participation stimulated our exploration of his method, which he named group analytic psychotherapy. He had the rare capacity to look behind any statement including those of his own which he had previously thought through carefully and written down. When groping for a concept I found his free associative discussion baffling. My impatience was stilled by the warmth of his friendship. He was not offering clarifying statements backed by his undoubted authority. Rather he wanted my observations, my re-phrasings of my perceptions and my abstractions from these. My grasp of what I had read, heard or discussed came first and wherever I wandered he would be there inviting me to consider our bearings. For him theory was not a recitation of well understood rubrics but the meeting of minds on negotiated territory at a particular time. The terms of the meeting might be to confirm concepts by all means, but immutability of them never. He taught me how to theorize rather than to memorise the current theories. He was a great teacher of method. This appealed to me because I saw method as useful in many contexts and enduring beyond the synthesis–dissolution–resynthesis cycles of theoretical structures. Yet Foulkes was not light on theory. He could trace the difference and the implications of these differences between his own position and those of Freud, Melanie Klein, Jung, Bion, Balint, Slavson, Perls and many who were his contemporaries. After all he worked at the psychoanalytic clinic in Frankfurt before the war. The practice of group analytic psychotherapy he developed in post-war England, though he acknowledged the earlier influences of psychoanalysis, the Frankfurt School of Gestalt Psychology, the Sociological School there and the ideas of Kurt Lewin and Goldstein, and the wartime so-called Northfield experiments concerned with battle casualties. The theory seminar method was the presentation of classic papers and key passages within a time of theoretical themes. The discussion led by two teachers for each year sought clarification of concepts. These were further clarified by anecdotes from the teacher's treatment practice.

Selection for groups and the setting for them, frequency and duration of sessions, the termination of treatment, the administrator function of the conductor, his analytic attitude, his note-keeping and evaluation, co-conducting, transpersonal processes in the group, the phenomena of mirroring and resonance, boundary incidents, various sorts of interpretations and conductor intervention, absences, holidays, fees and conductor defences were some of the themes of method studied.

As far as the exposition of theory was concerned, the elegance and clarity of Dr Malcolm Pines' thinking was memorable. The bewildering galaxy of concepts which I encountered on Pat de Maré's space ship voyage through theory[1] was breathtaking, but I could glimpse the complexity of philosophical, psychological and sociological concepts promising to be related to one another eventually. He bumped down to earth with the insistent reminder that I should pay attention to the influence of the context in which personal interactions occur.

Then James Home surprised me with philsophical ideas as fresh as April showers. In his paper 'the Concept of Mind'[2] he argued that Freud had regarded certain symptoms as having a particular personal meaning. It would follow that such symptoms are personal creations and not simply effects of causes. He conveyed to me an impression that an analytic group member was having a sort of Pilgrim's Progress. Reaching the celestial city would be when there is sufficient growth in understanding for the individual. This takes place in a group of people who respect his struggles and where meaning of experience is the great mitigator of pain and passion.

Earl Hopper, a later figure on the group analytic scene, introduced a vigorous style in the journal club. He traced parallel writings of sociologists to those of traditional therapists. By implication, academic backgrounds, other than those of the caring professions, would be relevant to training courses for would be therapists. His direction helped me with selected readings of Simmel, Marx, Giddens, Durkheim, Blauner, Malinowski, Mead, Anne Parsons and others. He delineated the differences and development of such theoretical concepts as alienation and dialectical process — illustrating from theoretical material through two centuries.

Regular scientific meetings with guest lecturers increased our awareness of current research and practices, as did reading the journal 'Group Analysis'. These were functions of the Group Analytic Society (London) to which all the course members belonged. The journal reports the work of Group Analysts in different part of the world, and provides a forum for a dialogue between correspondents. I was stimulated to read the relevant literature as never before.

Supervision

The supervision groups had a membership averaging four with a supervisor. Most course members had supervision in more than one supervision group over the time. In this way the styles and influence of several senior group conductors were made available to each of us. The small supervision group had a business-like atmosphere, different from that of the treatment group. The structure, too, was different, with a smaller number of participants, yet the setting was a similar circle of members sitting with a supervisor rather than a conductor. The similarities were evocative of the analytic group which assisted us to recall the atmosphere of the groups which we were conducting and there to discuss. Sometimes, this in turn would evoke a degree of role playing by the supervision group members of certain interactions of people in the group presented. By role playing, I mean more in the style of a radio play, for members didn't leave their seats. This occurs unpredictably, but when noticed it does portray well interactions in a group which is being reported on. A useful happening, for what was obscure becomes clear. The supervisor often noticed those interactions in the *Supervision Group* which replicated similar interactions in the *Treatment Groups* under discussion.

The procedure of presenting the conductor experiences in rotation contrasted with the free ranging discussion of the treatment group. The supervisor was questioning in attitude and introduced concepts of method and theory at times and through my relationship with him and the group as a whole I found that authority issues were often intense and exacting. Smaller group numbers, together with this procedure, left little room for hiding and encouraged active participation. It was important that the discipline of the supervision group could influence the conductor's experience with his own group which became amply demonstrated as regular reporting proceeded, providing feedback over a lengthy period. Second hand experiences reported led me to consider my own first hand experience, the conductor's counter transference. This contrasted with the treatment group where first hand experience was immediate. I could share the tribulations and joys of setting up my own treatment group within the organization where I was working, with its particular psychiatric context. It was fascinating to hear about many different settings from others. I was enabled to select themes from the complex information of my group sessions and present them to others in the supervision group, so as to get their impressions of how I was relating to my group. I became aware in this way of how I was intervening as a conductor and the consequences of this in the group. What I could grasp was some confirmation of what was suitable and better awareness and clarification of my mistakes.

This latter was useful for me but for others too, just as I could emulate some of their strengths or recognize my own mistakes when they were reporting. At times a blind spot remained, despite the supervision group discussion and when others could see what was obscure to me I would be prompted to talk this over in my treatment group to find some personal experience which had awaited analysis.

The training committee has reports from many sources by the end of a course to assist with the timing of their agreement to a trainee's qualification and membership of the Institute of Group Analysis.

I have written quite a lot about my teachers but I am just as indebted to my fellow patients and trainees. This statement is too bald to do justice to a truth which is an inevitable consequence of the methods I have described.

When the course ended, what remained were warm memories, firm friendships and the promise of competent practice and continuing development as a treatment group conductor.

Postscript – From Trainee to Trainer[3/4/5/6]

In consultation with the training committee of the Institute and a local steering committee, I helped to start the Midland Course in Groupwork and Family Therapy in the area where I live. This came to be equivalent training to the General Course in London. A twin course started in Oxford and subsequently there have been provincial Groupwork Courses in Cambridge and Manchester, organized in conjunction with the Institute of Group Analysis and staffed by qualified members.

References

1. de MARÉ, P.B., Perspectives in Group Psychotherapy. A Theoretical Background. 1972 London, George. Allen & Unwin Ltd.
2. HOME, H.J., The Concept of Mind. Int. J. Psycho. Anal. (1966) 47, 42.
3. LEAR, T.E., The Midland Groupwork and Family Therapy Courses. Group Analysis, (1978), XI/3 265-266.
4. LEAR, T.E., The Management of Envy in an Experiential Training Group. Group Analysis, (1979), XII/1, 49-51.
5. LEAR, T.E., Beaumont-Stevenson, F. Midland Course in Groupwork and Family Therapy. Group Analysis, (1979), XII/2, 169-170.
6. LEAR, T.E., Unstructured Large Group Learning of Boundary Phenomena. Group Analysis 1980, XIII/3 p. 164-168. Read at the 7th International Congress of Group Psychotherapy, University of Copenhagen 1980. Individual and The Group Ed. Pines Rafaelsen, 2, 289-294.

Larger Group Perspectives

By PATRICK de MARÉ

"One day someone will venture upon this research into the pathology of civilised communities."
("Civilization and its Discontents", Freud, 1930)

By the time "Perspectives in Group Psychotherapy" (1972) was published I had already recognized the self-evidence of applying the principles of Foulkes's group analytic psychotherapy to a larger setting:- "What does the future hold? I think it is likely to be concerned not only with small and medium sized groups, not only with the controversy over therapeutic community and community therapy, but with much larger psychotherapeutic groups with a membership of fifty to a hundred, conducted by several co-conductors, non-directive and aprogrammatic with tiered circular seating arrangements reminiscent of the amphi-theatre. In this situation group dynamics become extremely clearly defined and atmospheres, attitudes, ideas and ideologies make themselves evident not as cloudy, idealistic non sequiturs, but as definitive climates which can be seen as either impeding, coercing or prompting communication, and which themselves are the object of study. In these larger groups is more clearly seen the antithesis, the polarization of conscious and unconscious. The problem for the individual is the intrustion, in the individual situation, of the repressed unconscious. For the large group, on the other hand, it is consciousness that is in jeopardy, both for the individual and for the group's equivalent of consciousness, mainly communication and organization. The problem for the rudimentary large group is its mindlessness; not how to feel, but how to think."

During the same year 1972, Lionel Kreeger and I, at the Second European

Symposium of Psychotherapy held at the Maudsley Hospital, launched the first large group with over a hundred of the participants attending the conference; this stimulated considerable interest and was followed in 1975 by Lionel publishing "the Large Group" which contained articles by ten contributors. Since then there has been an almost total lull in interest in this subject. However, from 1975 onwards, Robin Piper joined me in setting up, not without delays, a median sized group of forty people, both professionals and clients, which rapidly fell to thirty and finally stabilized to round about twenty.

We were buoyed up by Freud's comment ("the Question of Lay Analysis"): "A future college of psychoanalysis would not only teach disciplines familiar within the medical faculties, but would include branches of knowledge which are remote from medicine and which the doctor does not come across in his practice; the history of civilization, mythology, the psychology of religion, and the science of literature. Unless he is well at home in these subjects the analyst can make nothing of a large amount of his material."

We soon realized that it was appropriate to contrast the specific features of the large group with the characteristics of both psychoanalysis and small groups and accordingly drew up the following list of larger group specific features:-

(1) The larger group of twenty and upwards to at least a hundred can be approached by the same principles as Foulkes approached small groups, i.e. single circle seating, aprogrammatic, non-directive, convened rather than led, with regular meetings and with attention to selection, to boundaries, to nonhierarchical, free floating dialogue, with an appreciation of the group matrix and the locating or mapping out of the social implications of disturbed thinking.

(2) Such a setting should be handled with the care to detail already seen in psychoanalysis and small group analytic psychotherapy. The larger group is as complex and sensitive an apparatus as are individuals and small groups probably more so since the intention to think must over-ride the desire to locate and express feelings. The emphasis is on socio-cultural learning not on psychotherapy. It is the micro-cultural, the group mind or the 'metastructure' that is being explored. In psychoanalysis the intrapsychic subtext and the dyadic text occur in an unchanging standardized setting which virtually excludes context. The transference relationship is interpreted against a context of reality which the person of the analyst represents. In the larger group this context is more broadly based against a continuously emerging microculture. Culture plays a central role; cultural as distinct from social. Individual symptoms become collectivised as subcultures which impede the flow of dialogue.

We discovered not only that the figure of 18-20 members appears to be the appropriate size of the next stepping stone in an approach to large groups, (the 'median group') but that concentric circles and the envisaged tiered seating is strongly contraindicated; also that conducting should be confined to one or two conveners, certainly not several since this leads inevitably, by the very nature of its structure, to uneveness in the flow of dialogue, and towards the formation of splinter groups within the larger structure.

Dialogue goes in the opposite direction to the subcultures by cultivating micro-counter-cultures from whose independent standpoint it is possible to explore not only the subcultures but the current macro-cultures of the surrounding society. It is empowered to do so by the very nature of the group's increased size.

(3) The larger number alters the quality of the situation which therefore manifests its own particular brand of special features. For instance the permissiveness and acceptance that Foulkes encouraged enables us to speak of such things as 'Koinonia', a Greek term denoting impersonal fellowship, which is an extension of this attitude. The free floating discussion of group association characteristic of his approach becomes expanded to a more comprehensive dialogue proper.

(4) Cultural changes take the form of transformations and transpositions as distinct from sublimations and transferences. For example the larger group is sensitive to social pressures prevalent as macrocultural assumptions of the surrounding society, whilst the smaller group, being more slanted towards the unconscious, more readily accepts therapeutic assumptions in discussion of such topics as homosexuality which, until recently, was treated by the surrounding macroculture as a criminal offence.

It might be said, that larger the group to begin with, the more primitive its response, so that the larger group displays features similar to the unconscious of psychoanalysis with a facility for splitting, projecting, introjecting, displacing, contradicting, mythologizing, regressing, distorting, being morally and ethically imbecile, pleasure orientated, dependent and timeless with a certain mindlessness and illogicality, but with the prime exception that in the large group there is the enormous opportunity for dialogue. A discrepancy arises therefore of being both primitive and unconscious on the one hand, but potentially sophisticated on the other, in that dialogue proper is able to confront the unconscious with characteristic logic, precision and definition.

(5) The larger group setting is frustrating, anti-libidinal and anti-cathartic of narcissistic libido and incest object choices, thereby generating primary hate. As long as it remains unstructured, the massifying or fragmenting by primary hate and the revenge motif operate manifestly through subcultures. If, on the

other hand, hate is contained it can become transformed into endopsychic energy and structure expressable in terms of dialogue, thinking and emerging microcultures.

Dialogue proper is then capable (by the nature of size of group) of bringing about cultural transformations different both from the psycho-biological familiocentric oligarchic hierarchy of small group structures, and from the current culture of the surrounding society.

Subcultures of the larger groups are meanings derived by the combination of projected ideas or part objects from individual members. These subcultures shape and mould the group matrix which in turn expands by growing microcultures invigorated by dialogue.

The primary hatred engendered by the larger setting is mollified by the gradual transformation of mutual hate into impersonal fellowship or *koinonia,* it runs a course entirely distinct from libido, ending up not in love but in friendship.

(6) Dialogue is tangential and analogic as distinct from the binary digital logic of the one-to-one dyad. It marks a different way of thinking and is lateralised rather than causal. It can bring about the humanizing of culture as distinct from the socializing of the individual.

(7) The larger group dialogue is thought-provoking and can transform the mindlessness of a mob to the highest levels of sensitivity and intelligence.

(8) Topics concern not only intra-psychic and subtextual unconscious conflicts, but involve contextual considerations, i.e. an array of social and cultural aspects which are part of the human situation — illness, death, class, race, politics, economics, philosophy, current affairs, religion and art, the handling of universal human emotions, and as such, are not treated as defensive ploys.

(9) In brief, the larger group is a microculture of society with the distinction that we can address it and be answered by it. It is the watershed between the world and the personal individual experiential mind. It has features of the unconscious mind with the unique quality of being like a dream in dialogue; it offers us the opportunity to humanize both society and individual concurrently.

(10) The larger group is the opposite of the hologram. In the hologram, if the large plate is shattered, each splinter has a complete picture of the picture on the larger plate. In the larger group each member, through dialogue, projects a total transformation onto a group microculture which in turn reflects back into the individual. As an example, in India the individuals representing the British Raj were stereotypes; they maintained a relatively uniform structure throughout a changing sociopolitical environment.

(11) The larger group behaves like a tree trunk to the branches and twigs of

smaller groups and individuals, both sustaining and being sustained by them.

(12) This gives rise to the sense of Koinonia which is the opposite to panic, a central issue in separation anxiety which constricts the free movement of the mind.

(13) The larger group's prime resistance is absenteeism, which can result finally in no group at all.

(14) The central anxiety in the larger group takes the form of panic, manifested in individuals as a phobic state, the extreme form of mental anguish. Mass formation and packing (as in wolf pack), and the intense revenge motif of mob violence constitute the group's equivalent of counter phobic measures.

(15) Mass formation is a mindless dyad of leader and led. Like binary digital logic, it is reductive unlike the totalizing analogue of conscious lateralized thinking.

(16) Applying unmodified principles of psychoanalysis and group analysis to the larger group is like "playing ludo on a chess board".

(17) It follows that dialogue proper is neither a reaction formation nor a counterphobic measure but constitutes a transformational process; it transforms mindlessness into understanding (verstehen), meaning (meinen) and outsight.

(18) In the larger group, therefore, we are, in struggling with dialogue, not only responding to the pressures of the reality principle and the gratification of the pleasure principle, but with establishing a third principle, that of meaning.

April 1983.

A Group-Analytic Perspective on Family Therapy

By HAROLD L. BEHR

It has become traditional in psychotherapeutic practice to regard family therapy and group therapy as two very different styles of therapy, grounded in different theoretical foundations and calling upon an array of different skills and techniques. While this is undoubtedly true to a certain extent, and perhaps inevitable in the face of the growing specialization of these two modes of therapy, it can also be said that there is much more overlap in terms of shared concepts than is generally acknowledged by practitioners in the field. This paper outlines some basic principles in family therapy viewed from a group-analytic perspective and states some of the important differences and similarities between family therapy and group therapy.

The first point which needs to be emphasized is the simple fact that the family is very much a group. The contrast between 'family therapy' and 'group therapy' which is enshrined in the literature on these subjects, and indeed in the separate professional networks, organizations and institutions which have grown up around these therapies, is misleading and creates a climate of separatism which does not fully reflect the reality of the situation. 'Family therapy' is shorthand for 'family group therapy' a term now discarded as cumbersome, and 'group therapy' is shorthand for therapy within an artificially constituted group composed, usually, of people who have not known one another before coming together for therapy. The term 'stranger group' is sometimes used to distinguish the latter group from a family group, and for want of a better adjective that term will be retained here.

The group-analytic contribution to family therapy

In his book 'Therapeutic Group Analysis' (1964) S.H. Foulkes[3] defined the three types of group with which group analysts might be concerned. These are: (1) The Functional or Work Group (2) The Life Group, and (3) The Group-Analytic Group. The second of these, the life group, he saw as the type of group in which "the members are vitally interrelated. It has no single occupation as a group but its members are interdependent as to the basic ingredients of life. This natural network, e.g. family or extended family is an important field for group-analytic therapy and research" (Foulkes 1964).[3] It is interesting to note that Foulkes chose not to designate this group the 'family group', preferring to create a broader canvas for planning the treatment of the individual in his native setting, and leaving the option open for creating a therapeutic network which might include the family but might also transcend the family boundary and involve others who were 'vitally interrelated' and therefore important members of such a therapy group. Foulkes recognized that the whole gamut of human reactions could be encountered in such a life group, and he saw that these reactions, including symptoms, could be interdependent, and that disturbances in the life group could be seen as facets of the multipersonal network of interaction. Change in each member of the network would react on all the other members of the network.

Although Foulkes adumbrated later developments in family therapy he himself experimented only tentatively in that medium. He was much more concerned with the third of his three types of group, the group-analytic group as he called it, which was essentially a small therapy group made up of some six to eight members who have had no previous relationship with one another. Working in such groups Foulkes developed and refined his ideas on group analysis as a form of group therapy with its own specific ethos and concepts. The group-analytic situation for Foulkes was primarily a social situation within which therapy could take place. All processes and interactions could be understood by reference to the situation and to its boundaries within which earlier experiences and attitudes would be reactivated. Patterns of relationship that were relatively stable and continuous, namely the structure of the group, could be altered by planned and deliberate interventions. In any therapeutic situation the group analyst would be attentive not only to the structure of the group but to the process of the group (the dynamic component of the group which is in constant flux and includes the reciprocal relationships and non-verbal and verbal communications) and also to the content. The group-analytic method would facilitate the gradual evolution of awareness of the ongoing patterns of relationships by the members of the group themselves.

In such general terms did Foulkes lay down a blueprint for the application of group analysis to a wide variety of therapeutic situations, including the family therapy situation. However it was left to one of Foulkes' associates,

A.C.R. Skynner, to develop a model of family therapy based on the group-analytic model.[5] Skynner regards his technique as essentially group-analytic because of the following features which it shares with stranger group therapy:

> "1. A simultaneous study of the part and the whole are not seen in any way as incompatible, nor is one seen as a denial or rejection of the other. The psychological structure of an individual and of his family group are homologous, isomorphic, and changing one must automatically mean changing the other provided the parts of the system remain in contact . . . The therapist therefore has to listen to and observe both the individual contributions (which will all have their separate meanings, when taken together in relation to the individual concerned) and the communications of the group-as-a-whole (disregarding who says what and taking it all together), constantly attempting to relate them and understand one in terms of the other.
>
> 2. The family, like the small group of strangers, is seen as possessing inherent potentials for constructive understanding and for facilitating growth and positive change, as well as for creating confusion and blocking development. The main task of the therapist is therefore seen, as in the artificial small group, as the facilitation of these inherent growth-enhancing factors, and the creation of circumstances in which they can emerge and operate effectively.
>
> 3. Though the therapist has a responsibility for leading the individuals composing the group, and so must accept a position of responsibility and authority in relation to them, the wisdom and understanding potentially inherent in the group-as-a-whole will exceed his own; he must therefore be attentive to, and respect, what it is telling him about himself, and be willing to be corrected by it." (Skynner 1976).[6]

These points highlight the fundamental similarities between the two therapeutic situations. In the family group no less than in the stranger group the therapist is working with a network of persons with its own group matrix, that web of communication and inter-relationships which constitute the common shared ground upon which all communications are located. It is this family group matrix which exists as the therapeutic medium and within which the therapist can facilitate communication and sharing, helping individuals to move from less articulate and more primitive forms of expression, such as symptoms, to more articulate forms of communication. The individual in the family is as much a nodal point in the network as he is in the stranger group; in the family, as in the stranger group, psychological disturbances are located between persons and not confined to the individual in isolation.

The first principle of group-analytic family therapy may therefore be stated as an awareness of and respect for the family-as-a-whole. This is the point at which, intuitively, most family therapists of whatever persuasion, have arrived. The family as a group is placed at the centre of therapeutic concern, which in practice has come to mean that the whole family is required to participate jointly in treatment sessions whether or not the manifest symptoms have emanated from one member of the family. When a patient seeks help from an agency in which network therapy is a respected orientation, and when it is judged that the patient might benefit from an initial family interview, the family therapist will draw a boundary around those members of the patient's family who appear together to make up an optimal unit of therapy. These in Foulkes' terms are the members of the family who are vitally inter-related and inter-dependent as to the basic ingredients of life, which in Western culture generally brings together those members of the nuclear family who are living under the same roof. Quite often there are obstacles in the way of bringing such a unit jointly to therapy sessions; the therapist may then share with the family his view of the importance of the family as a whole, thereby introducing into the therapeutic situation an expectation that at some stage the absent members of the family will become involved in the treatment. This might entail a considerable re-adjustment of expectations on the part of the family, and the therapist, as in any form of psychotherapy, will have to preserve a balance between respecting the patient's defences and influencing the culture in the direction of therapeutic change. In cases where it is unrealistic to hope that certain family members will attend therapy, the therapist continues to conceptualize the family as a whole and to work with those family members who are present helping them towards an understanding of the role played by the absent members in influencing the disturbance within the family network.

It is by no means a rigidly held tenet of group-analytically oriented family therapy that the family as a whole should always be present if therapy is to be successful. In the vicissitudes of clinical practice it is quite common for a sub-group of the family to make use of therapy with good effect; equally, it is occasionally beneficial for the boundary around the optimal therapeutic unit to be re-drawn from time to time, so that different members of the family may be seen at different sessions, either on their own (for instance an adolescent youngster) or as a sub-group of the family (for instance the parents). In some families the disturbance is such that the composition of the family group presenting itself for therapy changes kaleidoscopically from session to session; that too is a phenomenon which can be profitably looked at by the therapist and family together. It may be decided that one or more members of the family deserve quite separate opportunities for therapy perhaps in an entirely different setting such as individual psychotherapy, stranger group therapy, or couple therapy, and the therapist is mindful of the need to involve other agencies where appropriate, especially as much of his work in family therapy is likely to involve children.

Skynner (1976)[6] has provided theoretical guidelines for drawing the boundary around the therapeutic group by introducing the concept of the *Minimum Sufficient Network*. According to Skynner the social equivalent of the functions represented traditionally by the superego, ego and id, are dispersed to a greater or lesser extent over a given social situation. The minimum sufficient network in any situation is the psychological or social structure containing enough of these three sub-systems to make autonomous function possible. Skynner points out that where the three sub-systems are adequately developed within the individual to permit communication within the intrapsychic network to a sufficient degree, it may well be that individual psychotherapy is the appropriate mode of therapy. Where these structures have become dispersed among a number of people, the only autonomous system will be the group containing those individuals. The family therapist has an important task in monitoring the boundary around the minimum sufficient network, much as the group conductor in the group-analytic situation accepts responsibility for guarding the boundary of the group.

In addition to being aware of the family as a whole, the group-analytic family therapist has to be prepared to involve himself as a total personality in the therapy, irrespective of the particular strategies and techniques which he might make use of at a given moment in the therapy. "The key requirement in the therapist is a deep awareness of his own identity which he is able to sustain in the face of overwhelming, if transient emotional arousal engendered by encounter with profoundly disturbed family systems seeking to externalize their pathology." (Skynner 1981)[8] The group-analytic family therapist may feel impelled to behave and intervene in family groups quite differently to stranger groups, yet that does not mean that he has compromised his therapeutic integrity; he is the same person working in two different contexts, each of which calls upon his personal involvement in a different way. In both therapeutic situations he remains quintessentially the group analyst.

Some differences between Family Therapy Groups and Stranger Therapy Groups

The group analyst who practises family therapy will remain aware of the similarities between the two therapeutic situations, but he will also be powerfully aware of significant differences. It is important here to distinguish between the family group and the *family therapy group*. It is the latter group, consisting of the family group plus the therapist, which makes up the *Thera-*

peutic situation, and which is the appropriate group to compare with the stranger group therapy situation.

(i) *Formation of the group*

The stranger group is assembled by the therapist who selects individuals who have had no previous relationship with one another and whose personalities and psychological disturbances will vary from one member to the next. The therapist strives to balance the group by achieving a wide scatter of personality characteristics, "a mixed bag of diagnoses and disturbances" (Foulkes and J. Anthony 1965)[4] so that an atmosphere of diversity is created in which cross-transferences, mirror reactions and other group-specific phenomena occur and become available to therapeutic intervention. The therapist tries to avoid the isolation of any one of the group members by holding at least one variable in common, such as intelligence or educational background if the group is very diverse in terms of personality structure and range of disturbance. The therapist himself, though different from the other members of the group in his 'administrative' function, and hopefully to the extent that he is the least disturbed and most integrated member of the group, does not differ conspicuously from the other group members in many respects.

The formation of the family group, on the other hand, has begun well before the moment of therapy; the family will have grown gradually and organically out of an earlier network, and the current matrix will be patterned and well organized making intervention by a newcomer (the therapist) exceptionally difficult.

(ii) *The life of the group*

The stranger group meets only for the purpose of therapy; it was called into existence for that purpose, and it will disband after the task of therapy has been completed. There is no contact between the members during the intervals between the sessions. The family group, as Foulkes points out, has no single occupation, but it embodies within it the multiplicity of tasks inherent in family life – creating and providing an environment within which procreation can take place, where children can be nurtured and prepared for an independent existence, and ensuring that certain patterns of behaviour can be replicated and certain values and traditions transmitted from one generation to the next. For the family that comes to therapy, the therapeutic situation is a transient part of the life of that family group. The family will not only have been together for a long time before therapy, it will continue to meet between the sessions, and it will continue to stay together as a group after the termination of therapy. The family therapist is faced with a group which, if viewed from the perspective of selection criteria for stranger groups, could not be more badly composed: far from being balanced, it is a group in which disturbance is shared and collusive attempts made to preserve a structure which however uncomfortable is one which provides a sense of identity and keeps alive the feeling of being vitally inter-related.

(iii) *The therapist's entry into the group*

The central role of the therapist in the stranger group is diluted by the group-analytic situation which renders him one stranger among several others. In the family therapy situation the therapist is conspicuously the most different member of the group. In the group-analytic sense of the word *he is the deviant member of the group:* that is to say, he is the person on whom attention is likely to focus relentlessly until he can integrate himself into the group or until he is expelled from the group. The therapist is different to the other members of the family therapy group in certain important respects: he is the new member of the group; he is the only person who does not share the group's history up to that point; he is the only member of the group who does not participate in the group's life between sessions; he is the only member who will certainly leave the group at the end of therapy; moreover the therapist joins the group at a time of stress or crisis (when the group is referred for therapy) and it is he who attempts to introduce a different culture – the therapeutic culture – by influencing, through his interventions, the boundary and structure of the group. The therapist faces the family with the possibility of change at a pace and to a degree which they may find alarming, so that group anxiety and defensive manoeuvres will be increased. All this appoints the therapist to a central role to a much greater extent than in a stranger group. In the stranger group it is primarily the *group* which is new to the therapeutic situation; in the family therapy group it is primarily the *therapist* who is new to the therapeutic situation. The family lays great expectations upon the therapist, who has to work hard to demonstrate that it is the group as well as himself which can be effective. While the stranger group also lays expectations upon the therapist, it does so to a much lesser extent.

How a group deals with a deviant member

When an individual enters a group as a new member the structure of that group alters, and the process, the state of dynamic flux in which communication takes place, undergoes an intensification. There is an impetus towards absorbing the individual into the group. If the individual is able to communicate with the group the process of absorption proceeds; if, however, the individual or the group are functioning at a level at which disturbance (or difference) cannot be communicated, the individual is experienced as an irritant to the group and he becomes a focus of intensified activity designed to remove him from his position in the group. The group may attempt to move him to the periphery of the group, to isolate him and ultimately to expel him; or there may be an opposite tendency, to draw him to the centre of the group and to assign a role of importance to him. Both of these tendencies may occur sequentially in the same group, as is often seen when a poorly integrated group member is made the centre of attention or given a position of exceptional power and then driven into an even more isolated position and ultimately excluded from the group. The tendency to move the deviant member centripetally or centrifugally may be a slow and subtle one, or it may take place abruptly and explosively. Whether the deviant member is moved to the centre and invested with leadership properties depends largely upon the level of maturity and cohesiveness of the group at that point in the life of the group. A poorly communicating group, such as a family in therapy might be, is likely to invest a newcomer, such as the therapist, with powerful expectations to do good or harm. If the former, the family may unrealistically expect the therapist to achieve magical change and then when he has failed, expel him from the group, which means in practice that the family drops out of therapy; if the expectations are of a harmful or destructive nature the therapist will have to work equally hard to dispel them, and if he fails the price may also be expulsion from the group. In a stranger group each member has a different expectation of therapy, and there may be drop-outs when expectations are frustrated, but the therapy group survives. *In family therapy, if one member drops out, it is the therapy group as a whole which is in jeopardy.*

It can be seen, therefore, that in order to diminish his deviant status in the group, the therapist in the family therapy situation has to work more actively to foster communication between himself and the rest of the group. Time is not on his side, and the intervals between sessions, which in the stranger group provide the opportunities for translating the therapeutic situation into the wider community, may be used negatively by the family to re-assert cherished defences and close ranks against the threatening outsider.

Implications for technique in family therapy

The family therapist has a two-fold task at the beginning of his encounter with the family: he must get to know the family, and he must help the family to get to know him. The first relationship he will concentrate on will be the relationship between himself and the family-as-a-whole, as if that were a dyadic relationship, and the mainstream of communication will flow between the therapist and the family more than between the family members themselves.

Getting to know the family

The family will generally present itself with its disturbance crystallized into a symptom, and the therapist will take that as his starting point and determine where in the family's network the disturbance is located. A common pattern is for the disturbance to be located in one member of the family, typically a child who is nominated by the family as the patient. The family may hold a shared view of the child *as* the symptom, or they may see the symptom as residing *within* the child, for example a problem exclusively affecting a part of his body which is dysfunctional; they may for instance believe that a wetting or soiling problem reflects a disturbance of bladder or bowel in isolation from any other aspect of the individual or his network. Families functioning at a more integrated level of communication may locate the problem within a relationship. An example of this might be a family which recognizes that difficulties in the relationship between the parents are affecting the children and creating disturbance in other parts of the network. Some families are even at the outset able to acknowledge that the disturbance is located within the family network as a whole, and they are ready to let the therapist join the network and to communicate with him as the person who can help the family to change their own pattern of relationships. Other families come into therapy with disturbance located within the family's relationship to the outside world. The boundary between the family and the wider network may be the focus of disturbance, and effective therapy may need to involve, as part of the minimum sufficient network, individuals or agencies (e.g. a school) over whom the disturbance is dispersed.

Group-analytic family therapy gives equal weight to the here-and-now of the therapeutic situation and to the past. There is no implicit prohibition on the content of the material brought by the family to the sessions, and an investigation of past relationships is not necessarily seen as an evasion of current problems. To the contrary, the therapist may well have to journey with the family into their own past in order to gain a proper understanding of how the family came to develop their particular shared assumptions about themselves and the world. Some families might attribute their predicament to a single event located in their past, for example the death or departure of one of their members, or a move from one place to another; disturbance in one member may be traced to an identification of that member with a family ancestor who has come to be represented in the family mythology as the transmitter of undesirable traits, and so on. Much therapy takes place in a context of helping families to mourn the loss of significant others and realize the pathological investment in people and situations from the past which is impeding their free engagement with the real world. To do this work the therapist has to identify family myths and repeated patterns of behaviour.

The genogram is a specific technique used by many family therapists to elicit aspects of the family's history. Using a blackboard or sheets of paper the therapist and family together map out a family tree through a process of group association guided by the therapist. The genogram often illuminates unexpected patterns of communication within the family, themes which resonate through the family, and areas of ignorance within the family about its own identity, all of which become available to the therapeutic process. Family sculpting is another technique commonly used to discover the family's view of past, present and future relationships within the family. This is a technique which calls upon family members to make use of the physical space within the therapeutic situation by taking up positions in relation to one another which represent family attitudes and emotional constellations. Sculpting is especially useful as a way of involving children, and with families who are inhibited or intimidated by the therapeutic situation. A family's experience of one of the children silently moulding them into statuesque postures which reveal for the first time his view of the family, not only provides that family with new insight but frees them to talk about things which they may not have been able to articulate before. These techniques therefore open up the possibility for change as well as helping the therapist to get to know the family.

Engaging the family

There is no clear demarcation between diagnostic and therapeutic interventions in family therapy. The therapist is aware that before the end of the first session with the family he will have to reduce the family's anxiety in relation to the therapeutic situation to a point where they will be prepared to come back again or to accept the therapist's recommendation for alternative ways of helping them. The therapist who transplants a passive, waiting, non-directive posture from the stranger group situation to the family therapy situation is courting failure. In family therapy, much more than in other analytically oriented modes of psychotherapy, it behoves the therapist to attend to the courtesies of the social situation if he is to succeed in closing the gap between himself and the family. He is quick to introduce himself and give a full explanation of his expectations of the session, and he will respond briskly and selectively to the multiplicity of cues which the family will be offering him through their verbal and non-verbal communication. Family disturbance generally declares itself quite conspicuously early on in the session and the therapist may need to provide a counterbalancing influence by drawing the family's attention to his awareness of their strengths and assets as well as their shortcomings.

The presence of children in most family therapy sessions calls upon a special knowledge and understanding of the child's modes of communication. The therapist is careful to address himself to the family in language that the children will understand, and to involve the children (and the parents) through drawing, play, and conversation which links with the theme of the moment. Too often the therapist neglects to involve the children except in a token fashion, and the session evolves into therapy for the adults in the presence of the children (Dare and Lindsey 1979).[2]

Family members who have come along reluctantly, without seeing themselves as involved in the disturbance, have to be acknowledged as important participants and led towards an awareness of their own part in the family network. They may need to be helped to verbalize their resistance to coming and to be shown that their own perception of events and relationships is valued. The therapist will have taken account of each family member's rôle within the family and will have attempted to engage each member individually before the end of the first session. He will be alert to the possibility that some members more than others will be likely to undermine the therapy and cause the family to drop out of treatment. In families where one member is being scapegoated the therapist may have to be prepared to protect the scapegoat at the risk of alienating other members in the family, and if necessary to assume the rôle of 'scapegoat' himself, within the therapeutic situation as a first step towards providing the family with the powerful corrective experience that he is very different to the nominated scapegoat. (Skynner 1979).[7]

Longer term treatment strategies

The therapist moves from the symptom towards more articulate forms of communication within the family. The pace and depth of change is determined by the families as a whole, and the therapist has to be prepared to tolerate being put into a variety of different rôles. He may at one time or another find himself called upon to be a container for family disturbance, a 'switchboard' through which the family can safely communicate with one another, a surrogate family member, 'go-between' between family members or between the family and the outside world, and so on. Change can occur rapidly, and the results after even a few sessions are often dramatic. The therapist may choose to work out a contract with the family, limiting treatment to a number of sessions, or focussing on specific aspects of family disturbance (Bentovim 1979),[1] or he may, in other families, adopt a more open ended, free-associative treatment strategy. Family therapy sessions tend to end on a more resolved note than stranger group sessions, and this is as much by design as by chance, to militate against the re-assertion of family defences between sessions.

The therapeutic factors in family therapy are not easy to identify, but they are often surprisingly simple. For some families *the act of telling* is therapeutic in itself; sometimes it is the creation of a space within which communication can occur that is important; permission to express feelings; correction of distorted perceptions; discovery of new ways of communicating; all these are familiar to the psychotherapist and important in family therapy no less than in other forms of psychotherapy.

References

1. BENTOVIM, A. (1979) Towards creating a focal hypothesis for brief focal family therapy. Journal of Family Therapy 1, 2; 125-136.
2. DARE, C. and LINDSEY, C. (1979) Children in Family Therapy. Journal of Family Therapy 1, 3; 253-268.
3. FOULKES, S.H. (1964) Therapeutic Group Analysis. London, George Allen & Unwin Ltd.
4. FOULKES S.H. and ANTHONY E.J. (1965) Group Psychotherapy. The Psychoanalytic Approach. London, Pelican.
5. SKYNNER, A.C.R. (1969) A group-analytic approach to conjoint family therapy. Journal of Child Psychology and Psychiatry. 10, 81-106.
6. SKYNNER, A.C.R. (1976) One Flesh: Separate Persons. Principles of Family and Marital Psychotherapy. London, Constable.
7. SKYNNER, A.C.R. (1979) Reflections on the family therapist as family scapegoat. Journal of Family Therapy 1, 11; 7-22.
8. SKYNNER, A.C.R. (1981) Chapter in: Handbook of Family Therapy. Gurman A.S. and Kniskern D.P. Brunner/Mazel, New York.

Group Analysis and Higher Education

By M.L.J. ABERCROMBIE

The ideas of group analysis and ways of behaving in therapeutic groups have played an important part in my academic development. My experience began as a teacher of zoology in a fairly conventional degree course at Birmingham University, and continued with three research projects at University College, London. The first of these, supported by the Rockefeller Foundation for ten years in the Department of Anatomy, focussed on training pre-medical students in the skills basic to diagnosis. The second, in the Bartlett School of Architecture supported by the Leverhulme Trust Fund and the Social Science Research Council, was concerned with educating for a professional role in a rapidly changing society, which, among other things, would require working in design teams. The third project, sponsored by the University Grants Committee for three years, was aimed at improving small group teaching in the Universities.

It is perhaps at first sight surprising that my adoption of the ways of group analysis should have occurred during the first project, when the problem I was tackling was that of learning to behave scientifically in the practice of medicine. Observing accurately and comprehensively and drawing reasonable conclusions from the information obtained seems an objective, rational, individualistic activity far removed from the emotional conflict-ridden human relationships that are the stuff of group psychotherapy. The essential link is the students' and patients' relation to authority figures, and the way their past experience conditions their present behaviour.

Consider the process of observing. I had for some time been dissatisfied with the results of didactic teaching in biology, which was supposed to help students to be observant, but the weight of knowledge we provided seemed to inhibit the ability to see things as they really are, to distinguish what *was* visible from what they had learned to think ought to be visible. For instance a text book diagram of that simple microscopic creature, *Amoeba,* will show it to possess two prominent spherical organelles, the solid nucleus, and the contractile vacuole. This diagram is a composite picture of what can be seen in different conditions. In the living *Amoeba* the nucleus is difficult to distinguish, but the contractile vacuole is clearly visible, rhythmically swelling and contracting, filling and emptying. In the dead Amoeba, fixed and stained, the vacuole is invisible because it has completely contracted and the nucleus is prominent, because it has taken up more stain than the rest of the body. But often a student drawing an *Amoeba* will draw both organelles, whether the creature he is looking at is living or dead. In the same way a child drawing an apple through which a knitting needle has been thrust will show the whole needle as though the apple is transparent, drawing what he knows, not what can be seen. Nor do we adults always distinguish clearly between the words "seeing" and "knowing".

Accounts of the physiology and psychology of vision gave little help in understanding the phenomenon of observer error — of the same stimulus pattern being differently interpreted by different observers, even experts in the subject, and of the same observer interpreting differently the same stimulus pattern at different times. But soon I came across the work of Ames[9] and the advocates of the transactional aspects of perception (see, for example, Blake and Ramsay),[10] which vividly demonstrate the influence of past experience on seeing. I began to see that the difficulties of behaving objectively, rationally and effectively were in some way connected with the way the student perceived his own relationship to knowledge, through his relationships with knowledgeable people, and therefore with his authority-dependency relationships. The problem was, how to take advantage of other people's experience without being confined by it, how to use old knowledge to behave effectively towards new and unexpected experiences. I started to teach in small groups, playing a non-directive role in discussion, but this raised considerable hostility in some students. As a result of gossiping about this with a colleague, I was invited by one of Dr Foulkes' colleagues to attend his therapeutic group of skin patients. It immediately became clear to me that if I could establish the kind of psychological climate that I felt in this therapeutic group, most of my problems in teaching groups would be solved. I therefore joined a therapeutic group conducted by Dr Foulkes, and started to apply some of what I learned from him in academic work. This involved profound changes in the teacher's rôle.

The conventional model of the teaching-learning situation is based on the mother-infant relationship, a group of two, perpetuating the transference relationship. This is still the most highly prized educational relationship, as is exemplified by the employment, by those rich enough, of a personal governess or tutor, or, almost exclusively in Oxbridge until comparatively recently, of the tutorial system in universities. True, most of us are taught in classes, but the lines of communication are still mostly from the teacher to each individual, and even in the relatively adult set up of the lecture theatre, the teacher talks and the students listen and are not supposed either to talk, or to listen, to each other. The relation between teacher and pupil is necessarily asymmetrical. The teacher is an authority in his academic subject, and the student ignorant of it; the teacher is further invested with the authority of the institute, to which the student belongs only transiently. The teacher, as an examiner, may have powerful influence over the student's career and future. So the transference relationship hangs like a millstone round both their necks, mostly unquestioned and unchallenged.

Now the distinctive feature of Foulkes' variety of group psychotherapy is that he deliberately tried to release the conductor from the transference figure rôle, and to encourage the group members to resolve their transference relationships by interaction with each other as well as with him. This was by contrast with other psychoanalytically oriented techniques of group therapy in which the conductor analyses individuals within the group setting, or analyses the reactions of the group as a whole to himself as a transference figure. There is a useful analogy there with teaching in small groups organized for students to learn from their peers. The monolithic nature of authority can be modified, each will be learning about his own behaviour by contrast and comparison with that of his peers, instead of with that of his teacher only. Instead of seeing things (or failing to see them) from the viewpoint of the teacher only, he can see them from the various viewpoints of several of his peers, can judge the value of alternative interpretations and select accordingly, instead of swallowing (or rejecting) the teacher's version, the authoritative one, automatically and uncritically.

The main features of the course[1] that evolved over some ten years were as follows. The course was offered to pre-clinical students of anatomy as an attempt to train them to behave scientifically. It consisted of eight meetings, each lasting 1½ hours, taking place regularly in the same room and at the same time each week, and members of the same group of 12 attended (though the course was voluntary, absences were very rare). The ideological frame-work was set by a demonstration of some principles of perception and communication, which showed how two people, or the same person at different times, looking at the same thing, would experience it differently. Exposure of the essentially egocentric nature of perception gave quite a shock to would-be scientists! Observer error in science was shown to be subject to the same laws as govern perception in ordinary life. The factors affecting what was perceived could be considered under two headings – the previous relevant experience of the observer, and the context in which observations were made. The reception of information through the eyes was used to illustrate the processes involved in reception of information generally.

After this introduction, each session began with an exercise which was tackled individually for about ten minutes. Students were asked, for instance, to compare two radiographs, to analyse the published account of a small piece of experimental research, to discuss the word 'normal', or to write on 'classification'. Comparison and contrast of the individual responses to the exercise formed the focus of the discussion which followed. Individual differences were often very sharp – what one took for granted as an 'absolute fact' another regarded as an inference of questionable validity, and the next minute, on another issue, the rôles of believer and doubter might be reversed. A point which one student had seen as crucial another had dismissed as insignificant, and still another had simply not registered. Students were encouraged to speak freely and spontaneously in their own vernacular, not required to use the formal language customary in the debating hall, or when presenting work verbally to the teacher. The pace and style of conversation was variable, sometimes rambling and even seemingly chaotic ('You're the only polite one' an angry girl said to me 'you're the only one who stops talking when you're interrupted'). The non-linear style of the discourse made it possible for a student attempting to evaluate another's statement, or to justify his own, to express not only 'good reasons' but also personal associations which were not questioned by himself, but might be by others. In this 'free' or 'associative' discussion a student could learn how his own judgment in scientific matters had been influenced by powerful factors of which he had been unaware, and which he had been unable to evaluate. These factors ranged from minutia of the immediate context (e.g. the details of the layout of a research report) to deep seated, generalized attitudes about human nature, e.g. about the extent to which one had assumed that research workers could be trusted to report their work accurately, or editors to evaluate it reliably; or whether one thought that good research is not likely to be done by women, Americans or physiologists working in a genetics lab.

In the last three years of this project we gave tests of observation to students and compared the performance of those who had taken the course and those who had not yet done so.[11] The following differences were found between the two groups. Compared with students who had not taken the course, those who had tended to distinguish better between descriptive and inferential statements, to make fewer false inferences, to consider alternative inferences rather than confine their attention to one only, and to be less 'set', i.e., less inappropriately influenced in dealing with one problem by the experience of an immediately preceding problem. These results indicate that the course helped students to make more reasonable judgments in scientific matters. matters.

The adoption of this method of teaching requires a reversal of the teacher's rôle from that used in lecturing. In order to encourage the student to examine his own habits of behaving in scientific matters, the teacher talks very little, but listens attentively and shows signs of having heard; makes tentative and associative statements rather than authoritative or dogmatic ones; sets a pattern of contemplating, of considering the various implications of statements, of noticing consistencies and inconsistencies between statements, of indicating the relevance of apparently irrelevant statements, and in general helps to analyse the extraordinarily complex tangle of ideas, perceptions and expectations that contribute towards the making of judgments. Hopefully, increased understanding of one's own mental processes will help one to behave more effectively, in this case in scientific matters.

The same basic principle was used in the other two projects, with students of architecture,[2-7] and university teachers using small group methods.[8] Again a small group met regularly for $1\frac{1}{2}$ hours weekly in the same room, and the teachers (two of us collaborated in these projects) played a highly disciplined rôle. The focus for discussion, however, did not begin with a specific exercise, but was spontaneously generated by current events – in architecture, the organization of the course, work in the studio, problems of designing, team work, assessing work, examinations – and with the teachers, their experiences in group teaching.

It is perhaps worth noting that while in this work we are focussing on specific academic or professional points (unlike the situation in psychotherapy when the whole personality is the target) participants often reported more peripheral changes. A medical student, for instance, said he could now talk to the vicar, and others said that the course influenced their general philosophy of life; similarly, some teachers spontaneously reported that their lecturing improved, not only their small group teaching, and that they got on better with colleagues, not only with students.

To summarize, I have found that some of the basic ideas of group analytic psychotherapy can be usefully applied in higher education – for instance, the need of the teacher to withdraw from playing a dominating didactic role, to encourage interaction among other members of the group, and recognition of the power of the 'group situation' – the sometimes apparently irrelevant features of the context that may profoundly influence the behaviour of the group. It is the style of conducting the group that matters most, and the rigorous self-discipline that is required can be most easily learned, I believe, by experiencing a therapeutic group for some time. It is important, however, to be clear about the boundaries between therapy and academic teaching; the non-verbal behaviour may be very similar, but the verbal behaviour is not. The best way of continuing to learn how to conduct groups is, I believe, to belong to a group of colleagues doing similar work, meeting at regular intervals to exchange experiences.

To facilitate the attitudinal changes that are necessary in teachers and students alike, it is a great help to study together video or sound recordings of their own classes. They can become sensitive to subtle clues that they were formerly blind to, and respond more appropriately to them. They can see how they collude with each other unconsciously in behaviour that reasonably they do not want to encourage. Students can slowly learn to outgrow the crippling effect of their dependence on the teacher,and find ways of monitoring what goes on in the discussion themselves – encouraging a silent student to open his mouth, for instance, or an over-talkative one to shut his. They can get better control of their own behaviour, and enjoy the freedom of doing better the piece of work they came together to do.

Acknowledgements
I am deeply indebted to the late Dr S.H. Foulkes and the Group Analytic Society, London, for inspiring the development of this approach, and would like to express my gratitude to Professors J.Z. Young and the late Lord Llewelyn-Davies of University College, London, who encouraged the work in the Departments of Anatomy and Architecture respectively, and to the Rockefeller Foundation, the Leverhulme Trust Fund, the Social Science Research Council, and the University Grants Committee, whose financial support made it possible.

References and Further Reading

1. Abercrombie, M.L.J., 1960. The Anatomy of Judgment. Hutchinson. Penguin 1969.
2. Abercrombie, M.L.J., 1966. 'Educating for Change'. University Quarterly, 21. 1. 7-16.
3. Abercrombie, M.L.J., Forrest, A.J. and Terry, P.M. 1970. Diploma Project 1968-69. J. Architectural Research and Teaching, 1. 6-12.
4. Abercrombie, M.L.J. and Terry, P.M. 1971. 'The first session: introduction to associative group discussion.' In Abercrombie, M.L.J. Aims and Techniques of Group Teaching, 2nd edition. Society for Research into Higher Education, 30-54.

5. ABERCROMBIE, M.L.J. and TERRY, P.M. 1973. 'Students' Attitudes to Professionalism.' Universities Quarterly, 27, 465-474.
6. ABERCROMBIE, M.L.J. and TERRY, P.M. 1977. 'A contribution to the psychology of designing.' J. Architectural Education, 30, 4, 15-18.
7. ABERCROMBIE, M.L.J. and TERRY, P.M. 1978. 'Reactions to change in the authority-dependency relationship.' British J. Guidance and Counselling, 6, 82-94.
8. ABERCROMBIE, M.L.J. and TERRY, P.M. 1978. Talking to Learn'. Society for Research into Higher Education.
9. AMES, A., 1955. An Interpretive Manual for the Demonstrations in the Psychology Research Centre, Princeton University, Princeton University Press.
10. BLAKE, R.V. and RAMSEY, G.V. 1951. Perception – An Approach to Personality. The Ronald Press Co.
11. JAMES, D.W., JOHNSON, M.L. and VENNINGS, P. 1956. 'Testing for learnt skill in observation and evaluation of evidence.' Lancet, ii, 379-383.

Group-Analytic Psychotherapy in the Setting of a General Psychiatric Practice

By H.G. TOUGH

What potential exists for the coming together of group analytic psychotherapy and general psychiatric work? The former might be seen as a specialized closed system, the latter as concerned with less complicated therapies. However, in my experience there is a plasticity in each which makes possible firstly a co-existence, and beyond that a complementary relationship. Some consideration of my individual work situation and view of group analysis will clarify this statement.

As a psychiatrist within the National Health Service, I offer treatment to a specified catchment population in a semi-rural area in the Midlands of England. The work situation extends through an acute in-patient unit, a day hospital, out-patient clinics, emergency visiting of patients in their own homes, and professional consultation with a variety of other disciplines. Much time is spent in the supervision and organization of the work of individual professionals and teams, so that opportunity for the exercise of personal treatment skills comes to be highly prized. The variety in the work, changing demands, and fluctuating resources with which to meet them all, encourage an orientation towards change and experimentation. The trend locally and nationally is towards greater expectations of patients in therapy and to an increasing extent to stress the importance of autonomy, more responsibility for the self, and thus the need to become actively engaged in their own treatment. The treatment milieu, therefore, readily accommodates group psychotherapy in a variety of modes. The rôle of the psychiatrist can be very flexible and highly reflective of individual style, though on the basis of a core identity.

The situation of the group analyst might be similarly viewed. The training with a focus on the classical analytic group provides a basis which must needs be modified when application is attempted in the variety of opportunities presented in the 'back home' work situation. Perhaps it is better to conceive of a core identity serving as a basis for growth. To paraphrase Foulkes[1] the group conductor who merely learns a rôle and who cannot develop will fall back and fail. The identity of the group analyst is also affected by the relationship between Foulkes and his theories on the one hand, and the state of organization of his theories on the other. His personality and theoretical approach are closely intertwined – this point is stressed in the evaluation of Foulkes by graduates of the Institute of Group Analysis[2] when his personal qualities as a therapist are emphasized. He presents in many ways the ideal therapist figure and modelling oneself on this seems sometimes more helpful than attention to theory. This modelling process is highly personalized and is likely to be quite variously manifested in terms of style. When one considers his theories these are said to be relatively unsystematized – this is both a drawback and strength. The lack of closure gives scope for development and especially for individuals to use group analytic theories in a way which is appropriate to their particular creativeness.

Given the narrowest of definitions of the practice of group analysis, one would have to view the rôle of the group analyst as secondary to other functions of the general consultant psychiatrist. However, if one considers the broad foundation of group analysis, its acknowledgement particularly of the importance of Gestalt psychology, social psychology, Lewin's field theory, the relationship of the individual to the matrix with its implications for individuation, the salient principle of treatment *by* the group, the stress laid on communication (widening, deepening, making verbal), then a wider view can be taken, i.e. that group analytic principles are capable of application to a variety of organizational and group structures with issues of treatment, education, leadership, and social engineering. With this wider view, the psychiatric and group analytic functions can be complementary. There are, however, issues requiring particular consideration.

The non-directive analytic approach is not suitable for all patients. Some patients, particularly in the in-patient situation, manifest extreme dependency, e.g. the neurotically regressed, psychotic or deeply depressed categories. With these patients, the group conductor requires to be more authoritative and generally more active than usual to avoid unduly raised levels of anxiety. This makes the later phase of diminished conductor activity described by Foulkes more difficult to achieve and group development tends to be slow. An element of didactic reality testing may be required, for example, for several sessions a middle-aged depressed patient had ignored her fellow group members and made persistent demands on the group conductor – though very wearing, these demands were tolerated for a time but eventually it was pointed out that she was functioning like a small child with a parent. She received this with an acute display of anger but then for the first time became active and involved with other patients.

Family practitioners are the main referral agents. They are generally accepting of group therapy. Quite often patients have been frequent surgery attenders and resistant to help at this primary care level, as well as to simpler psychiatric treatment. The close and often lengthy engagement with these patients in group analytic psychotherapy affords relief to the family doctor. The focus away from medication, the patient's assumption of personal responsibility for his condition and treatment, are also welcome, and offer a fresh perspective on therapy. The relationship with the family practitioner has a powerful effect on the patient's attitude to group entry. He may have difficulty in letting go, so that the patient has to work through divided loyalties. At the other extreme, a negative relationship may be manifested with the more complaining patients who then come to the group feeling rejected. This can result in hostile feelings ('doctors are all the same') or in simple relief and the expectation of a better experience ('thank goodness; it was such a strain'). Some family practitioners load the patients with excessive expectations ('I have the greatest confidence; I send my patients nowhere else, etc.'), and this accentuates feelings of disappointment later on. The more symptom and medication oriented patients maintain contact with the surgery for a time; after that they tend to resort to the family practitioner only for intercurrent ailments or in moments of crisis for additional support. Resumption of formal contact with the practitioner nearer the end of therapy is clearly bound up in the issues of ending and individuation – there is a great deal of reluctance on the patient's part; depressed feelings may be expressed, and contact may be made abruptly or unexpectedly, as though personal initiative were under test.

After this experience, some family practitioners will refer further patients specifically for group work so that the culture is gradually modified. Cultural attitudes are very important. The community as a whole holds conservative attitudes towards psychiatric treatment and towards group psychotherapy in particular. Interestingly, group therapy becomes more acceptable when it is part of a larger programme of treatment as in the day hospital; it is as though the threat of the group is diminished if authority is seen ultimately to lie outside it in a hierarchically superior organization. There may be several issues in this. Some patients have particular difficulty in assuming personal authority, with others there is a splitting off of superego function from the group, as though the group is an illicit area of release; others desire to avoid problems or fear that the group will prove an inadequate container for these.

One has to recognize, however, cultural social reserve. This can be a drawback; the developmental aspects of group analysis make possible the extension of help to those with life problems rather than psychiatric symptoms. Such patients are slow to present themselves to family practitioners and are unlikely to be referred unless presenting with neurotic symptoms or acting out behaviour.

It is interesting also, to note the effect of a growth-oriented approach on an essentially caring and illness-oriented treatment culture such as the National Health Service. My own experience is that this latter can add an attitude of social dependency to the group situation and later on this can affect the ending of treatment. Some patients have a limited awareness of the total treatment in the locality while others may have had previous contact with other types of psychiatric care. They might by virtue of this fact alone be deemed to be likely to require long-term support. On the other hand I think that some of these patients may find it difficult to distinguish the psychotherapy group from other parts of the system of care, i.e. that any point in the system may be regarded as a phase rather than an end in itself; termination from the phase may not be synonymous with termination from the system. Work in the group is then attenuated by the exception of a move to some other therapy; the tomorrow is the defence against today. While further treatment may be deemed inappropriate, it can be difficult to avoid offering something. Where a defined period of alternative therapy may be offered, for example, a period of individual support, this can be extended through pressure from the family doctor, the patient, or relatives. Referral to a junior colleague, if possible, carries the implications of failure, and rejection. Underneath the personal issue may be therefore a problem of contract – the therapy contract is not only made with the group therapist but also with the system and in the case of the latter it is open-ended. The private treatment contract is advantageous in being specific and closed. In this area the general psychiatrist has a different experience from the consultant in psychotherapy who will be recognized as offering only a specialized service and be able to refer back to psychiatric colleagues if other forms of therapy are required. A somewhat similar issue can exist with medication where the group conductor may be expected to accept responsibility as he would with other forms of therapy. It is expedient, therefore, before accepting a patient, to establish that the general practitioner or another psychiatrist, will assume that particular responsibility.

It can be a problem for the psychiatrist to maintain opposing frames of reference. I have in mind particularly the contrast between the decision-making specialist on the one hand, and the non-directive group analyst on the other. The willingness to explore and the receptiveness necessary for the group analyst are inappropriate in settings where reassurance and limit setting are the requirements. Balance becomes all important and the maintenance of appropriate boundaries is a major task. Absolute containment is not realistic or desirable; cross-fertilization is necessary for the psychiatrist to maintain an internal consistency and if integration of concepts is to be explored. The work then is concerned with monitoring of important boundary crossings and the state of permeability of the boundaries. Stress on the psychiatrist can be substantial. Also too much may be expected of very sick patients and not enough of the more capable. Pressures from one context may be worked through in another. The group analytic setting can become a relief for the conductor from other pressures — it may become a particularly rewarding experience with the risk of a mutually satisfying group culture which is undemanding of the therapist. On the other hand an awareness of therapist rôles can act as a safeguard against excessive emphasis on technique; a more natural manner on the part of the conductor can allow greater contact with the group. Under these circumstances authority and responsibility are more readily accepted by the group. This is not to be confused with abdication of authority as a reaction to the exercise of it outside the group. Nor is it an opportunity to make premature or unrealistic demands for group maturity. Rather, it represents an awareness of the authority inherent in consultant psychiatrist status and the need to avoid reinforcement of this and undue enhancement of the transference.

Co-conducting is not only useful for training purposes but in feedback and self-evaluation of the conductor's rôle. Different frames of reference exist; the co-therapist is likely to be quite junior or from another discipline with a different training and educational background although perhaps having had an acquaintance with group analytic technique. Within the therapy group the conductor and co-conductor may exhibit differing styles with the resulting degree of confusion — I have learnt with particularly inexperienced co-conductors to use their interventions for a better understanding of the group process as much as any free association of the group and at times to comment on them as with a patient's intervention. Provided this is not taken to the extreme that his every remark is capped and rivalry feelings stimulated, I have found co-conductors accepting. If carried out in reverse, it provides the group-conductor with an opportunity to examine his rôle as a group member as well as therapist. In post-group discussion a different frame of reference offers a challenge to his own set ideas. All in all, the presence of a co-conductor makes the conductor more vulnerable, more sensitive, but hopefully potentially more valuable to the group. This is not an advocacy, however, against solo conducting; co-conducting entails more work and discomfort and in my own situation is used in a minority of groups and largely for training purposes.

Much of my own work is on a crisis level with individuals, couples, and families, often in the home setting, and in partnership with some fellow worker such as a community nurse, social worker, or junior colleague. Quite often a domiciliary consultation takes the form of an impromptu one-hour family group with a diagnostic aim though sometimes producing change or enabling the family to decide whether they could cope within their own resource. There are a small number of in-patients – as community resources have developed these patients increasingly represent organic, psychotic, borderline and severe personality syndromes. Most represent short-term crisis admissions who will return to the community in a matter of weeks. There are also medium-stay and long-stay patients, largely schizophrenic, awaiting either a community placement or transfer to a chronic ward. For the most part they will all receive traditional care with some emphasis on milieu. However, in recent years all the in-patients under my care plus staff members have met in a weekly group of anything from twelve to eighteen people. The group has a limited continuity from week to week. The orientation is group analytic though greatly modified and much concerned with recurring themes, e.g. acceptance of the individual, the admission crisis, authority issues of the in-patient situation, the relationship of these to the outside community, the translation of symptoms into life problems, the analysis of group association, and with the introduction of activity techniques and didactism at times. The aims are to educate the staff by providing understanding of the effect of the ward environment on patients, to help patients and staff to examine common issues, and to enable both to relate in a less rôle-bound way. It becomes increasingly difficult to distinguish education from therapy. The mix of patients makes for a conglomerate of topics with marital crises from newly admitted patients ranking with problems related to money, cigarettes, food, etc. raised by psychotic patients. Schizophrenic and borderline patients tend to lock one into a narrow, often persecutory rôle; positive action by confrontation and reality testing is needed to help the patient recognize this. These patients on discharge tend to need supportive group therapy in the day hospital setting. In the in-patient group they have a complementary relationship with the neurotics, offering up areas of disturbance for examination by sometimes discomforted neurotic patients; the neurotics will at times take on a helping rôle towards them and are in turn helped to mobilize their ego strengths. The large staff presence can be unwieldly but it does mean that the total unit culture is represented in the meeting and this minimizes the possibility of conflict between the group culture and the larger unit ethos. Also, the staff are encouraged to consult with each other across the meeting and with the patients so that the psychotic and borderline patients have an opportunity to identify the staff as individuals and to counteract the tendency for them to fix on one member as representative of the whole staff, or to relate to all staff in a homogeneous, indiscriminative way.

There are a variety of other groups – weekly out-patient group analytic groups for patients and professionals in training, a multi-therapist assessment group within the day hospital, a staff group and a community meeting. There is a large in-service teaching commitment including a psychotherapy seminar for junior psychiatrists, conducting experiential groups in a formal group work course, and a supervision group for group therapists.

Teaching is a great encouragement and reinforcer. Apart from extending one's own knowledge and having an opportunity to re-think ideas, it is gratifying to give in a direct way which is not appropriate to group analytic therapy. I consider this opportunity, along with support from one's colleagues, and a life situation where satisfactions outweigh dissatisfactions, to be important for the group conductor's well being. It is not simply a matter of maintaining a status quo, and the more complex issue of personal growth must be considered. One can learn from one's group patients by observation and empathy. Also at times problems brought up by patients stimulate the conductor to work through a conflict of his own within himself. This is an experience which brings one into intimate contact with the group and has a different quality from that of 'moving out' and disengaging from the group in moments of introspecting on the group. I can feel grateful for this but also at times guilty and vulnerable which I take to reflect a degree of therapist omnipotence making it awkward to receive from patients. However, the lack of opportunity to share this with the group and acknowledge whatever help one has received is felt as a deprivation and on these occasions one can feel disadvantaged compared to patients and wish to have a patient opportunity oneself. This, of course, may transcend personal issues and reflect something of a group's avoidance and resistiveness to containing all its problems.

There is a cluster of issues related to the discreteness of the Health Service catchment area which requires consideration. There is a correspondingly restricted selection of candidates for group therapy and those presenting are not always very suitable. However, despite this, early drop-outs seem no more frequent than elsewhere. Therapist transparency can be a problem through knowledge of the therapist from other treatment venues though this is not very intrusive. There is also the question of intervention by relatives facilitated by geographic proximity to the treatment locale – spouses can become prominent in crises and directing them to help to another colleague can be resented by them. Perhaps it would be an advantage to include spouses in the pre-entry contract interview so that boundaries can be defined with them at a time when they are more open to co-operation. More significant and long-lasting, is the possibility of patients developing extra group contacts through sharing the same transport either deliberately or inadvertently, arranging social meetings or as a group conducting post-group inquests. The destructive effect of this on the group process need not be elaborated on. What should not be overlooked, however, is the possible element of constructiveness particularly where there is collusion by the whole group which may say something about cohesiveness, power-taking by the group, and the exercise of initiative. All resistance is not antitherapeutic.[3]

In considering the diverse patient populations worked with in different situations and the changes in pace and orientation required of the psychiatrist, one must acknowledge the possibilities for scapegoating, splitting and projection by the psychiatrist. When demands in all areas are minimal then the variety appears to present little problem. Pressures, though, generate tension which is liable to spill over into other areas of work, particularly in my experience, with a greater impact on the management of those groups with highly dependent patients. The caring rôle rather than the analyzing one seems to be the more difficult to sustain under pressure. These latter patients by virtue of their demands and relative helplessness, more easily provoke feelings of rejection or detachment on the part of the group conductor. It is as though in these groups the sense of group identity is most fragile, the group boundary weaker, more reliant on the conductor for its maintenance, and more permeable to outside influence. This is in contrast to the experience of groups with more autonomous patients when the feeling is of enclosure, the boundary is monitored by the group members, and the group is less reliant on the conductor. Presumably therapists working solely in group situations would encounter the same syndrome in moving between groups at earlier and later stages of development.

The emphasis in this paper has been on relating group analysis to the local community and to the larger treatment system. This is very needful. After all, my patients' awareness of boundaries should be matched by my own.

References

1. Foulkes, S.H. (1975) Group Analytic Psychotherapy — Method and Principles. Ch. 7. London. Gordon and Breach.
2. Graduates of the Institute of Group Analysis Evaluating Foulkes' Work, 'Group Analysis', Dec. 77, X/3, 241-243.
3. Schafer, R. (1973) The Idea of Resistance. Int. J. Psycho-Anal., 54, 259-285.

Group Analysis Related to Social Work

By VALERIE MALLON

A training in group-analytic psychotherapy can enhance certain personal characteristics such as persistence, creativity and accuracy in approach to a broad spectrum of work. Further, it provides over a prolonged period an opportunity to experience and observe intriguing juxtapositions within groups. This is akin to noticing the artist who paints a favoured model into many pictures, but so varied in detail as to be unrecognizable until one learns to look for such detail and to observe in a certain way. So in the group-analytic experience one learns to observe the individual (and oneself) in different guises within various groupings. One may, as in the art world, be said to develop the eye and instincts of the connoisseur. In some respects this developed sense of analysis of detail can be as uncomfortable as it is rewarding. The observation would take account in the picture of the relatedness of story, content, colour configuration, history, depths, background and inner communication to the viewer.

In a study of the nature of groups and of psychotherapy, Foulkes and Anthony (1965)[2] say "The fact that all the disturbances that we ever seek to treat by psychotherapy or group psychotherapy stand out significantly as disturbances in inter-personal relationships cannot be merely peripheral and accidental." They draw the conclusion that this indicates the presence of factors of central importance and what is suggested basically is that the significance of *Relatedness* in all aspects of life is shown up with greater clarity in the group-analytic treatment of people with neurotic disturbances than is apparent in other more conventional groups.

Foulkes and Anthony (1965)[2] go on to say *"Relatedness, seen as taking place within a basic all embracing Group Matrix, is the corner-stone of our working theory."* To draw a parallel, our curiosity may be aroused about the 'relatedness' of artist, pictures and model as we become aware of the special attraction and influences at work when the same model is used by the artist many times to represent different people. Once the mind's eye has, through training and exposure, become aware of and familiar with the phenomena of group-analytic psychotherapy, it becomes easier to see and work with relatedness in situations in which the aspects are less clear as, for instance, in family groups or in day-to-day social work. This leads me to consider the benefits which may result from a stronger partnership between group-analytic psychotherapy and social work practice in that social workers have relatively free and privileged access to people in their home, work, residential and other situations, who are experiencing neurotic disturbances. This could provide a rich source of material for study and analysis in new territory at the boundaries of health and social care. In return, social workers would benefit from training in group-analytic work in order to develop a more scientific approach to social group work.

Social work, being in large part an active, diverse, sometimes parental, and essentially practical occupation concerned with people and environment as interacting systems, has little time for connoisseurs, and in many ways this is its most refreshing, challenging, yet frustrating characteristic. In reality, being something of a specialist in group work and especially in group psychotherapy may be of little immediate value to the social worker, other than in a personal sense and as an important point of reference, until there is recognition of opportunities in unlikely aspects of practice. It was interesting to find during a colloquium for members of the Institute of Group Analysis (London) that each in our different professional field had experienced initial frustrations and feelings of impotence as newly-qualified group-analysts.

Another interesting experience shared at this meeting was the use of imagery concerning material for analysis. It seems that we draw on early professional study experience in the process of analysis, so that someone who had been a scientist had the image of a laboratory with slide and microscope for detail examination. My own early study experience had been in art school before a career in social work, which might explain a preference for picture images for close examination. This raises interesting questions about images in early treatment and leads also to curiosity about the images of other professional workers.

It may be noted here that social workers tend to seek specific techniques to be applied to areas of specialism, so that there exist islands of applied social work each with its own culture, language and taboos although within one social services department. This is to say that certain techniques become the prerogative of a complexus within the organization, e.g. the Child and Family Guidance Service may hold a prerogative to train in and practise family therapy. Intermediate Treatment Centres and specialists (IT relates to work in the juvenile delinquency field) tend to favour behaviourist and psychodrama techniques, but view analysis of any kind with suspicion. Workers with the confused elderly lean towards reality orientation training and so on. It is interesting to speculate about images and earlier experiences in relation to these preferences. Whilst these techniques have obviously developed for sound reasons and often provide a good tool for the work in hand, there is something to be said for a 'thinking skills' (Ann Hartman – 1981)[4] dimension to enhance more active techniques and to provide umbrella coverage for exchange and sharing of experiences, which would lead to a range of skills and techniques being available to suit individual client needs. It is often quite fortuitous that an individual or a family is referred to one centre rather than another, and yet this determines the nature of the work offered. This may not be flexible enough to suit the client's needs at a particular time or feel personal enough to engage him-her in treatment.

In one psychiatric out patient clinic, (Lear, Bedi and Mallon – 1976)[5] where there is a group-analytic orientation, it seems possible to negotiate treatment with patients on a wide basis to suit the circumstances. At the same time this flexibility is contained within an overall analytic framework so that the negotiations also provide useful material for analysis. Part of this flexibility arises from the multidisciplinary and voluntary participation in the work of the clinic by the various professionals, which reflects the group-analytic approach to work and training. The process is complex, but basically means the nurses, doctors, social workers and psychologists contribute different professional skills and expertise and in return learn experientially the fundamentals of group-analysis, along with a developing 'thinking skill' dimension which can usefully be applied to all aspects of main stream work. An example of the assessment and treatment processes and range of options is as follows:

A young married woman was referred by her general practitioner to the consultant psychiatrist in whose clinic he had occasional sessional work. The patient was subsequently referred to the psychiatric registrar (co-therapist in my group-analytic group) and myself with a view to assessment for group treatment. The patient turned down an early afternoon appointment and further scrutiny of the notes revealed a suggestion that she had some difficulty in getting out by herself. She kept a late appointment and was brought by her husband, along with the two young children. It became apparent that this woman had a severe problem in leaving her house, and any treatment for her would be almost impossible to arrange for this reason. She had had an unusual and traumatic upbringing through living in another country at times with relatives, whose primitive culture was totally different to that of the east end of London where her parents lived, and aspects of this early experience could be related to her present difficulties. She desperately wanted treatment and to us sounded interesting and a promising group member. However, she was stuck and we had to work hard to avoid being drawn into this 'dead end'.

We were able to offer family therapy sessions as a means of loosening the situation, as a preparation to long-term treatment and as a means of confronting the woman's double bind. Further, the small children appeared pale and under-stimulated as they did not get out much, and through my social work contacts it might be possible to interest the mother in a local playgroup — she had trained as a nursery nurse. These shifts in the context of treatment and extension of work outside the boundaries of the clinic are contained within a group-analytic framework, with all the material being available for analysis within the treatment sessions. This amount of flexibility is possible because —

(1) the consultant psychiatrist is a group-analyst and tutors the general practitioner in this approach to consultation,

(2) my own training relates to — an analytic child care training/social work experience;

—family therapy training;

—training as a group analyst;

(3) as a training experience, the psychiatric registrar is co-therapist in my group and equally interested in a co-therapy opportunity in the family therapy sessions offered.

Another example of the range of options for treatment in the group-analytic out-patient clinic concerns a couple recently living apart. The wife lives in the matrimonial home with the children, whilst the husband has obtained accommodation attached to his place of work. The wife sought the help of the general practitioner as she feels miserable, isolated and afraid of her feelings of pent-up anger in relation to the children. There does not appear to be a significant other attachment for either husband or wife.

As part of the assessment and negotiation process, and following a visit to the wife by the consultant psychiatrist, an appointment was offered for husband and wife to attend the out-patient clinic within a few days. Both attended together with their delightful baby of about one year of age and I discussed with them the difficulty of coming together to the appointment. Having explored the situation together in family sessions it became possible to suggest and negotiate treatment opportunities for each. The wife is offered weekly individual sessions as an initial step towards long-term psychotherapy, probably later in a group. The husband offered to look after the children and to let her have the car so that she can get to the clinic. The husband became interested in the personal and professional gains to be had from membership of a group-analytic training group and he would be offered a place in a few months time. At a later stage it may be possible to offer this couple conjoint therapy or a couples' group experience, if this is appropriate.

I felt able to share my personal experience of having been patient and professional in training in the group-analytic situation, as this seemed appropriate to the exploratory sessions with this couple. It is my impression that 'transparency' on the part of the therapist is a significant enabling technique in group analytic work, in that patients get a glimpse of something realistic which may be hopeful and interesting, as in this instance, or which may accurately describe their own unexpressed feelings, bringing a sense of sharing and usually some movement as a result. This technique is perhaps potentially useful within the social work context, where it may be used with particular effect because client and social worker boundaries are more permeable than in many other professional relationships. For this reason, however, the analytic training and framework assume a greater significance within the less structured context of general social work.

At this point, I paused to look up a Foulkes (1975)[3] reference to metaphor. En route through his book, "Group-Analytic Psychotherapy, Method and Principles", it is rewarding to find a comment in the opening paragraphs of "The Conductor as a Person and His Training" – "His interests (the conductor's) should be of a more detached, sublimated kind similar to that of a scientist or artist."

Following on from the concept of relatedness within the group matrix as the cornerstone to group-analytic working theory, one might similarly describe relatedness within the network group or plexus as the cornerstone of social work. Thus, I suggest that what is learned and applies through a study of the working model of group-analytic psychotherapy equally applies to the wider context of social work. Besides the inner work which is the main concern of the working model, and arising from this, there develops a keen sense of boundary awareness and of structural inter-relationships. This factor is probably of most consequence to the social worker concerned as we are with the individual or family in relation to their environment.

In the context of group psychotherapy, Yalom (1970)[6] describes the possibilities for training group and individual therapists drawn from other professions and allied sources so that, as he says "The past decade has witnessed the demise of the concept of psychotherapy as an exclusive domain of psychiatry. A short time ago therapy was indeed a private affair. Psychologists were under surveillance lest they be tempted to practise therapy; social workers could do 'casework' but not psychotherapy." He is, of course, here describing the American experience and goes on to mention successful programmes for training housewives, psychiatric technicians and college students to do psychotherapy. It seems to be well accepted now that many people have a natural flair as therapists and others learn rapidly. Indeed, group patients in varying degrees become therapists as part of the process of learning through treatment, and this process is also central to the group analyst's training.

There are, however, other considerations in psychotherapy which are perhaps more particular to the group-analytic psychotherapist. These are concerned with the awareness of matrix, boundaries and of material, so that minute particles of something of potential value can be picked out and set within an appropriate context for analysis, similar to the scientist studying minute particles on a slide with the aid of a microscope. In group-analytic psychotherapy, all these processes take place within the context of the treatment session. In group-analytic training groups, however, it is possible to analyse material outside the group in a wider context with theoretical references to assist in the study of the subject. Then to return to enrich the treatment matrix with this deeper understanding. Problems here relate to distraction and group boundary management for the therapist.

Foulkes and Anthony (1965)[2] say that "Our need is for a dynamic science of psychotherapy, which uses operational concepts and which is studied, formulated, and applied in the actual process of therapy. It will study the process of change through clinical observation in the therapeutic situation, fully accepting and exploiting the idea that therapy is research and research in this field is therapy." It may be that the group-analytic idea of one process for research and therapy offers a model for training for the autonomous social work practitioner so much desired by the profession. The trainee group-analyst is required to bring into play his prior professional knowledge, group skills and previous life experience. These may have to do with boundary keeping of patient/client information, records, communication and alternative treatments, or to do with practical arrangements of space, time, permission, trust, colleague involvement, tables, chairs, reception, consultation and other aspects (all familiar arrangements in social work). At the same time the trainee is learning the new skills connected with group-analytic psychotherapy. There is, too, the patient selection process for the group, which has much to do with boundaries. Finally, there is the central process of the conductor in the group and the analysis within the group and outside the group; in the clinical supervision setting.

The description of therapy programmes given by Yalom, wherein therapists are minimally trained, suggests that the analysis and other parts of the total process such as selection of patients takes place within a wider context than the group. This is similar to the training process described, in that the treatment of patients with a group-analyst in training actually takes place within the wider context of the Institute of Group Analysis. In effect this split process describes the method of work in general social work, where social work supervisors/managers traditionally have boundary keeping functions in relation to social workers. Sometimes evaluation or monitoring is carried out by a research team who are either internal or external to the organization.

In order to be successful in group-analytic work in the wider context, it is necessary that a sense of relatedness exists and that boundaries and context are agreed and worked over in such a way that the material is able to be 'ploughed back' into the group like a good compost. It has been my experience that group analytic work enables one to develop boundary awareness — personal, inter-personal, group inter-group, and in relation to systems and networks.

At a practical level, I can relate a simple personal experience of boundary conflicts. I had to take over the domestic arrangements for a workshop suddenly at overnight notice. The building was strange and so the location of tea, coffee, cups, milk, keys and hot water was compelling. In addition, I had to make up groups and conductors according to final numbers attending. It is no under-statement to say that I was quite enjoyably busy with these practical arrangements until a request came for me to leave the domestic scene and to attend the conductors' planning group. This brought a sudden and effective feeling of being rescued. I had quite failed to notice the point at which one or two members of the workshop were already filling the gap in the domestic situation.

This makes me wonder whether administrative management and practice vested in one person are compatible functions within the same context. It is possible, also, to relate the experience of being rescued to the social work context where it is necessary at times for social workers to be rescued and given permission to leave the practical dispensing area in order to develop an exploratory and analytic approach to the whole range of work, including what *is* going on in the kitchen.

The rescue experience is echoed in the therapeutic session in the freeing of the 'stuck' patient (or family) by therapist or group permission to alter a pattern. The experience is one which may be observed with great clarity in family therapy work. In fact, permission to be still and thoughtful in social work is almost wholly reserved for formal training programmes, for research or development work, and for specialist practice, which does not help to bridge the gap between learning and practice in generic social work. As Ann Hartmann (1981)[4] says in her article (based on C.A. Alexander's idea of the territory between knowledge and practice).

"One of the activities that lies between knowledge and practice is thinking." At the same time, I value greatly the 'cut and thrust' pressures of mainstream social work in this country in which social workers are able to have a basic, honest, sharing and privileged relationship with clients and to experience with them many of the problems and real frustrations in everyday life. This is close to the group conductor/member interaction in group-analytic work. The analytic tool can, however, be a safeguard against collusion with self-defeating behaviour which is often experienced in social work. This tool can also be used to open the door to creative improvizations which bring a sense of enjoyment to the most arduous work.

It is exciting to discover that the creative yet technical aspects of the group-analytic approach have an affinity with business management techniques as, for example, in a recent social work management workshop* where analysis of material was central, as was the use of groups. The language and equipment were different but enjoyable, and the theory was familiar, with references to systems theory, de Bono, etc. Similar links can be made with other therapies and techniques, especially in the family therapy field.

In some respects one might speculate on group-analysis and social work in the same way as the 'How to swallow an elephant' riddle. The images of large shapes, powerful bodies and omnipotence are quite compelling in their possibilities. There is a real similarity in the answer – 'spoonful by spoonful' – in the small but significant areas of work which go on almost unnoticed. In a management capacity which provided the opportunity, I was able to use the review session of a child in residential care differently by introducing an element of analysis of material. A familiar sense of frustration with the review process led me to offer some ideas about our information and then to engage the girl herself in the analysis, with surprising results. I was able later to write up the experience, which made the options clearer and demonstrated the alternative routes in the process, as follows:

There appears to be a choice of route in the process of reviewing the circumstances of children in care –

(1) A motorway route, which fulfills in management terms the requirements for providing an efficient, routine system to cover statutory obligations and enable files and records to be up-dated. In fact, this route takes account of a great many of the real needs and functions of the organization.

or

(2) A country-road route, which is longer, slower and has interesting

distractions en route. In this instance, the girl's inner wishes to become a nurse were more clearly understood. (Her mother had died in a psychiatric hospital in curious circumstances, her father has a progressive muscular illness, the social worker from the past to whom she is most attached now works in a hospital setting and her ex-housemother's daughter is a nurse as is her father's present wife.) A similar exploratory excursion with the girl revealed also that she longed to have a foster family, which had not been understood. In fact, the reality of successful placement in a foster home is probably unlikely, but at least the links for opening up discussion with the girl about herself and her family now exist, and she probably has a sense of being more accurately understood.

I notice as a psychotherapist that I tend to have overall more sense of awareness of significant personal detail than as a social work manager, prior to training as a group analyst. It is also interesting now to have an overview and to attempt to reconcile the conflicting goals which are apparent at middle management (i.e. operational) level, whilst at a higher level of senior management the goals seem to be more idealistic and straightforward. For example, at a higher level the child care review system is quite simply to achieve good standards of social work practice and to make the best possible provision for the child. At an operational level, family, houseparents and social workers begin to weave fantastic webs of collusion. This collusive element was apparent in the example quoted in the common wish to get the job done well, but not to disturb anything; a good example of the reflective processes whereby management tends to get the response required for the smooth running of the system and there are no rewards for interrupting this arrangement.

It is suggested, however, that a balance of accuracy between management and practice *is* rewarding in that a client's inner wishes and ambitions are at least understood, so that more accuracy in planning is introduced at an early stage rather than that plans are ineffective at a later stage as they do not reflect the longing of the client. For these reasons, and drawing upon my own experience, I am of the opinion that social work management and group-analytic training and practice on a sessional basis go very well together and enrich each other. There is an opportunity to experience conflict, to analyse the problems and to arrive at more accurate and realistic decisions at interface work between management and practice.

In another instance, it was possible to analyse and write about a series of double binds in the department arising from trade union advice not to fill in for other people in a time of enforced cutbacks in staffing. What to do at the inter-face with clients waiting at an unmanned reception desk? This could be related to the many double binds in which clients involve unwitting social workers. A quote from Bateson (January 1970)[1] seems appropriate to the context — "There is a larger Mind of which the individual mind is only a subsystem." It is interesting also to relate this to the Foulkes' concept of the mind as a group process rather than an individual structure. Both have an intriguing relevance to the complexities of social work. It is often unclear in social work which mind we select as individuals in our professional work and especially when messages are conflicting, as happens frequently in general social work. Accuracy in assessment and creativity in response are valuable personal assets to draw upon in tight corners.

The response which occurred to me in relation to the two conflict situations mentioned was to produce a new journal within the department for the purposes of writing about practice experience. The style was taken from the journal 'Group Analysis', in which there is free expression and analysis of events as they happen within this field. Foulkes (1975)[3] says "The principles which govern our activities in group-analytic psychotherapy operate mutatis mutandis in a great variety of important situations and other tasks in life itself."

In reality, I have to cross a bridge from social work into psychiatric territory in order to practise group-analytic psychotherapy, and to cross yet another bridge to become a tutor/conductor to an inter-disciplinary course in group work and family therapy. There is a generosity of spirit at both ends of these bridges, but it would be rewarding to see more traffic crossing over in both directions. There is another shorter bridge which does carry more traffic, and that is towards family therapy work. Here, the language is similar and there is understanding of detail analysis. Increasingly, however, I am aware in family therapy work that the group-analytic experience adds an additional dimension to family therapy techniques. Apart from the basic group-analytic concepts of psychotherapy and research within the group-analytic context, there is a strong structural dimension which, like good scaffolding, provides a secure platform for family and workers on which to build confidently or to attend to repair work. This dimension comes from the careful constructs of group-analytic theory and practice, and allows much scope for therapists to share their range of professional skills, when appropriate, with the family as part of the matrix experience. When the work is complete and the therapists remove the scaffolding, the family structure remains with the now manageable internal work continuing to engage the family.

There is a noticeable sense of mutual respect between the therapists and family within this context in which group-analytic structure is used. It feels possible to reach out to patients and also to use a variety of techniques experimentally to suit the 'in situ' circumstances. This allows for treatment in a most realistic way and takes account of less than perfect treatment conditions. A group-analytic structure used in this way provides a boundary and a sort of compass to help steer one through the uncharted seas which lie between the continents of health and social care.

The application of group-analytic theory and practice is a realistic proposition for most aspects of social work, as it is essentially concerned with relatedness and boundary analysis within the different but related cultures of health care and social care. The exploratory and pioneer work together take place in the seas between, where there are more than enough people waiting to be rescued or given aid as to choice of direction, as well as those who would like to join in the voyage of discovery. During my voyage through this paper, I have discovered a new interest and focus in the spaces in between – theory/**/practice, practice/**/management, health care/**/social care, specialism/**/ genericism, treatment/**/training, and so on. There are those group-analysts who have pioneered work on the most difficult and hostile of territories, for example in work with people who have an alcohol dependence, in work in the most secure units of the psychiatric prison and in work with disturbed adolescents. There are many areas of more fertile soil waiting for such cultivation in territory outside health care which, if worked, might well reduce the pressures within the overloaded health care units. This work requires permission and patronage to establish a new culture in the field of preventive social/medical care.

Conclusion

Throughout this article, I have been aware of a gradually unfolding scene which reveals the absorbing, struggling, and maturing process of integrating within myself the group-analyst and the social worker. To some extent, as may be recognized, I still feel like a 'displaced person' in professional terms, and perhaps this discomfort is a necessary adjunct to change. As a balance to this, however, a new sense of accuracy in assessment and response brings rewarding comments from colleagues and, at times, from patients. As if they wave from the shore to encourage me on my journey, with the hope that I may return with something of interest and wonder.

The central theme of 'relatedness' described by Foulkes and Anthony enabled a circular exploration of new territories, leading to comparisons and linkages. The concept of the territory between theory and practice and the idea of the 'thinking skills' model for social work brought a sense of relief and familiarity. I wanted to say to social workers – this is what group-analytic theory and practice, (relatedness within a group matrix) has to offer. A structure within which thinking skills can be nurtured and allowed to develop.

In summary, the group-analytic model offers to social work an integrating experience and an atmosphere conducive to the development of thinking skills in order to link theory with practice. On the other hand, I believe that social work can remind group analysis of the centrality of the family group, linking our personal experiences with professional experiences. Further, because social work is a diverse and active profession it tends to be distracting and to interrupt proceedings with fresh information about people in the community. This causes a looking 'upwards and outwards' to see what is going on in society and in its relatedness to individuals. This, in my experience, can be a welcome corrective exercise for the group-analyst whose customary posture is to look 'inwards and downwards.'

References

1. BATESON, G., Steps to an Ecology of Mind. Page 436. Paladin Books.
2. FOULKES, S.H. and ANTHONY, E.J. (1965). Group Psychotherapy: The Psychoanalytic Approach. Harmondsworth. Penguin Books.
3. FOULKES, S.H., (1975). Group-Analytic Psychotherapy: A Method and Principles. Page 172. An Interface Book: Gordon and Breach.
4. HARTMANN, ANN. Social Work, January 1981. The Family: A Central Focus for Practice. Page 11. National Association of Social Workers, Inc.
5. LEAR, T., BEDI, A., MALLON, V. The trainee and Group Experience, Group Analysis (1976) IX/3, 208-216.
6. YALOM, I.D. (1970) The Theory and Practice of Group Psychotherapy. P. 100. New York: Basic Books.

*The Manchester Business School — Creativity Programme. (George Lester and Frank Lucraft).

An Application of Group-Analytic Principles in Pastoral Training for Clergy

By F. BEAUMONT STEVENSON

We thought we would do it differently.* For many years, pastoral training for theological students has been taught with an emphasis on learning counselling skills and doing a basic group work training – the idea being that if you put future clergy in groups they generally learned how groups worked which would be of some value to them in their parishes where there were all sorts of committees and gatherings. It was also felt that the other members of the group would give them feedback on their behaviour increasing their skills as pastors. We felt it wasted some of the opportunities which were available for exploring much wider issues: for instance the relationships between belief and action, what happened as a group of Christians formed their own community (would it be any different from any other community, how would it formulate its purpose for existing, handle disagreements etc.). What could be discovered about the "group mind" – the "sense of the meeting" as the Quakers so aptly describe it. Could we establish a form of belief laboratory in which the beliefs of the group collectively as well as those of its members individually could be inferred, studied, perhaps modified from gesture, words, unconscious action and compared with the *supposed* belief which the student said he had at doctrine class. We already observed that unless theological thinking could be practised under conditions of stress, the student was likely to regress to pre-theological education views in times of crises. On one occasion during one of our sessions, a 'phone message came through for one of the students from his home about a crisis involving a death. The meeting almost broke up as students panicked and looked for a "priest" to help with this "real" issue. When we reflected that they had pastoral responsibility for each other and they probably had the resources to help, they could look at some of the

*Michael Moran and the author.

assumptions they had been acting on and see that their well-polished views were forgotten during the crisis. The question was how to practise theological thinking under fire, as a medical student uses his knowledge under the battle conditions of internship, to see what was actually there and what could be learned.

Within my group analytic training I was aware of several processes which were described in analytical terms similar to theological dynamics described in applied theology. The question was, were they the same? Also the intriguing thought came up that if beliefs might be systematically analysed, could these be applied to discovering the beliefs of psychotherapists so that patients who were exposed to an intimate relationship with their therapist could at least have the opportunity of knowing what particular belief they were possibly about 'to catch'. This was made aware to me at the time by a friend of mine who had just been 'converted' within the context of the Freudian analysis. He seemed to have found insight into all the nuances of his past except the 'religious' one in which like the new convert, his beliefs were that all the problems of the world could be solved by people being indoctrinated into the new faith by undergoing an analysis such as his. I was also aware that I may have undergone the same process myself and of course would have probably been the last to know if I were doing so. What we both needed was someone who was aware of the nature of belief systems and their impact and limitations to help reflect this to me. Many clergy are only trained in their own doctrinal belief system through which they look at life and fit the pieces they see into their own system without necessarily being able to discern another's belief system as an entity in and of itself. Other clergy are trained to discern belief systems and are able to reflect the foreground pattern of behaviour against the background of the belief tapestry. They can therefore give help to those not in their own system of belief. To give an example, one of the popular current belief systems is the 'scientific' one. As a belief system it can be contrasted to scientific enquiry as such. Scientific enquiry seeks to see things as they work as objectively as possible. The scientific belief system is to dress up knowledge so that it looks scientific and is acceptable to scientific scriptural canons (usually statistics). Hence most psychology is written in obfuscatory professional language with many graphs showing undoubted 'proof' of the way things are. Since statistics can usually be arranged like scripture to come up with any conclusion the author wishes to present, it cannot rightly be said to prove anything. Suffice that the canon of statistics has been invoked, the experience is therefore 'valid' because it has been shown to conform with 'canon'. Similarly scripture presents the entire continuum on most issues from "forgive your enemies" to "drive the unbeliever out of your midst". It is precisely this ambiguity of scripture (and statistics) which makes it useful in looking at the profile of the belief of he who invokes it. We usually invoke only those parts which support the way we believe and conveniently brush aside the rest. Therefore in listening to the believer quoting scripture or the scientist quoting statistics, we listen for the distortion of the balance of things. S.H. Foulkes called this: "Locating the disturbance within the group matrix". He also pointed out that it was revealing which events were arranged as foreground and which were background. Most groups will tend to present all sides of an issue (from sympathy to confrontation) with much in between. We therefore listen to the weighting to look at the resistance within a group. A group may cluster at the cuddling side or on the kicking side. Similarly, a religious person may present a "bulge in the carpet" by distorting the balance of forgiveness-judgement continuum on the judgement side. He quotes hell-fire and brimstone, is tight-lipped and rigid. The distortion in the profile of the belief system he preaches covers the pathology beneath like a carpet lying over an object beneath it. There is a bulge under the judgement section, a dip under forgiveness and compassion. The belief system and the pathology beneath it may interact with each other in that the distorted belief system may re-inforce the distorted personality pattern beneath it even after the personality has changed.

In groups certain themes recur. Listening to where an individual is stuck, or what he is pre-occupied with, brings up the beliefs or assumptions which are present either within the individual or which he is 'catching' from a larger group or system to which he belongs. In family therapy the model is made that the sickness in a family may not come out through its sickest but its weakest members. Tracing it back and having the sickest member own his own feelings may help 'cure' the weaker members. Within the training of the theological students we should see various events of the theological college being acted out in the courses. The difficulty of integration of two colleges was reflected in a split within the members of our small group; the Principal leaving the college was paralleled with the leaving of one of the group members "under a cloud".

At Harvard, Paul Tillich used to demonstrate this same pattern of belief manifesting itself in art. He maintained that art mirrored the philosophical/theological thinking of any patricular age. He showed slides of works of art and compared it with the current philosophy of the time. For instance, in the renaissance period when man was emerging as the dominant interest, the paintings showed large figures of faces of people with small trees in the background. (In the picture of the Mona Lisa one can just make out a few insignificant trees in the backbround). In the age of Rousseau, when nature was emphasized, it was reversed . . . tall trees, small people. Here background and foreground were reversed. After World War I came cubism, where the familiar forms were still present but broken up from their usual shape. Art is a visual barometer of the belief of an age – the fact that there is no universal prevailing form of art today reflecting the fact that there is no world-view which is shared by all. Perhaps the fragmentation helps show the individual differences more closely than if there were more universal schools of thought.

In a much similar way a group will paint a picture in its themes, reflecting its 'group mind' moving now this way and now that like a flight of birds who fly collectively with one mind. Through all of the given contributions of each member there nevertheless run common themes. For any given group, certain things remain in the foreground – others in the background. This is probably more observable in family therapy where certain patterns of a family's characteristic will emerge over a given time. "Hostile feelings are never shown in one family" or "no room for tender feelings" in another. No better example than the apocryphal one of the woman during Queen Victoria's reign who was heard to say after the curtain had come down on the bodies lying all over the stage at the end of a performance of Hamlet "How unlike *our* royal family!"

Listening for the 'tune' or theme behind the jazz enacted in a group is the work of a group conductor; listening for a profile of the composer behind many interweaving themes is the work of the theologian. Such questions are: What is its religion (i.e. ultimate concern)? What priorities does it keep in the foreground when all else remains as background? Does it see its world as being something to be trusted or to be fought?

It is an interesting speculation to apply this same observation to what is happening in the world at the moment, looking for common themes running through the evening news broadcast or in the paper. It seems to me to be on the one hand a new renaissance in spiritual interest (meditation and discovering things human) and on the other a holding to ransom where smaller subgroups hijack planes, embassies, coal production etc. and hold the larger society to ransom. You may like to try the exercise for yourself using this morning's newspaper.

Application

The question arose as to how we could best arrange a setting in which to study these belief systems operating and to enable the future pastors to work with them. We felt the best thing to do would be to enable the theological students to construct and live in a world of their own design and observe, criticize and change it from the inside. What we did was to arrange for the students to meet with the conductors before the training exercise to design and set up the perimeters of this world. They were asked to formulate their reason for meeting together. They were asked to set the agenda and then to take responsibility for it. After an introductory exercise they were asked to state what their own pastoral questions and concerns were – to say where they were at the time. Out of these ideas, which were placed on sheets of paper, we designed together a common purpose for our life together from this. We reflected not only on what we wanted to study but also the things that were conspicuous by their absence. The interesting thing was how their interests frequently paralleled happenings in the college. Some groups centred around death and separation (as when the principal left the college) others around reconciling opposites (when two theological colleges formed into one). Some only wanted to discuss psychological issues and leave theological issues to one side. For others psychology was peripheral to an exploration of the risk of "being" in a world where rôles were demanded.

We met in a medieval manor house in a beautiful setting in rural Oxfordshire. A place which was a Quaker retreat house but was one of the oldest continually inhabited manor houses in England (complete with ghost we were told). A further chapter might be required to explore the possibility of a ghost as uninvited group participant (conductor?). Usually there were two groups of ten people who each met collectively for certain parts of the programme and for meals and then separately to do their own work. Each group had devised its own purpose, yet met together under the same roof to form with the other group a Christian community to celebrate the Sacrament together. When agnostic group conductors were present the issue of how to include the other was worked out. To begin with we posted up the purpose we had created together. This was discussed and any changes made on a collective level. If any individual did not feel he could commit himself to that purpose, he was allowed to go home at that point. A commitment to work together on that purpose was asked for. No one was allowed to sit on the fence – it was either 'in' or 'out'. Once committed, the group then began to form itself into a community. To begin with each member sat in a circle and shared with the others his own history – how he had come to the point where he was now – and what was important to him. Each was free to share what he wanted about himself but the variety of backgrounds reflected the fact that each had his own journey and had come to that point with different backgrounds and presuppositions. In the light of each history, the evolution of individual outlooks became more visible, various strands and themes became evident within an individual's life running into the life of the group. Parallels and distinctions between members of the group began to emerge within the choices and priorities which each had made in deciding to enter the Ministry and the way he had met the experiences of his life.

The groups divided their time among Applied Counselling Groups and Relationship Study Groups, theory and exercises, as the need for them became apparent. During the Relationship Study Groups we employed the use of doubling-technique used in psychodrama. In this, someone who brought in a written account of a pastoral encounter from his parish placement would write it up in verbatim form. As we re-enacted it, various members would stand behind the persons playing the rôle of the counselled or counsellor and speak for him with his hands on his shoulders. The idea was to get to the feelings behind the words. At a later stage we decided to 'quadruple' (or double the doubling) i.e. to explore the theological concern behind the feeling. Such a 'quadruple' might be 'I can't find any meaning for my own life, so I'll ask you to live my life for me and give it meaning. I am looking for a second-hand existence." We then reflected on how the concerns in the relationship studies were also repeated in their own relationship with each other on the course. Other exercises to help in this process were to write out an account of the Last Supper as if it were written as a verbatim by the apostle John, and studying it as any other verbatim; this included 'doubling' for Jesus' empty chair, especially toying with the possibility that Jesus could have asked Judas to betray him. Also time was programmed for solitude and meditation. During the Eucharist people brought objects signifying relationships which were important to them and presented them at the offertory at the Eucharist thus helping them come to terms with the use of symbols and the creation of sacramentals between people.

Upon occasion we have had a second part – this exercise which is composed of clergy who have been on courses in the past and who now are ordained and have parishes of their own. It is on this level that group analytic principles are more evident on a societal level. Rather than just presenting a pastoral concern, the priest presents 'his parish' complete with maps and charts showing the factions and subgroups and how their interests and concerns interact with each other in the context of the whole. What priorities and themes emerge, what changes are going on inside himself and how he is influenced by the wider groups to which he belongs and how possibly they are influenced by him. This is possibly more useful in England than it would be in the States in that parish responsibility here includes everything within a geographical area and not just members of one's own particular Church. The aim is to enable the priest to discern the conflict and development of different belief systems, for it is by belief that each of us live and find our meaning, it is also an area that remains largely unconscious even in the most aware of persons. To discover one's own beliefs from observing action and priorities, dreams and choices, is also to face the shock that we find our beliefs lie in different areas than we thought. Even the agnostic has that which he is tied down to (religature) and is on his own journey; he may in fact be the most religious of us all in his openness.

In writing this paper I have purposely left a gap. I have kept to the descriptive and not invoked either the scientific canon of statistics nor the spiritual one of scripture to justify my approach. It would be interesting when you read this to see which (if any) of the ideas ring true to your own experience. What criteria would you have appealed to to justify them? What authorities would you have quoted? What statistics cited? What examples would you have used – from clinical data, literature or scripture? What questions has it begged? Constructing these might be an interesting exercise towards formulating the canon of your own belief.

Application of Group-Analytic Psychotherapy to those with Sexual Perversions

By ESTELA WELLDON

My training in group therapy started in Medical School, when our Professor of Psychological Medicine conducted a group of his own students, who met weekly for three years. This experience gave me insight into the relationships between intra and interpersonal processes. Later, when I had students of my own, I was able to use this knowledge in order to improve my teaching. We started an out-patient service that offered therapy in groups for adults, adolescents and children. All of us concentrated on interpreting the dynamics of the "here and now", limiting our attention to the basic assumptions described by Bion.[1]

These experiences proved invaluable when I began work in therapeutic communities, first at the Henderson Hospital, where I was influenced by the work of Maxwell Jones,[2] and then at the Paddington Centre for Psychotherapy. In both centres, all therapy was given through groups, and we emphasized the importance of the community as a whole.

In 1971, I began to work at the Portman Clinic. For the first time, I was able to employ group analytic therapy in an out-patient setting which did not make use of the patients' 'community' as a therapeutic agency. I came under the influence of the British School of Group-Analytic Psychotherapy, founded by Foulkes.[3]

The Portman Clinic deals exclusively with patients who engage in acts of delinquency or criminal behaviour or who suffer from sexual perversions. Before I describe how I work with such patients in groups, it would be in order to discuss several important aspects of these very difficult patients. It is essential to realize that sexual deviance differs from sexual perversion. As Stoller[4] has argued, "The term 'perversion' is necessary – not withstanding its traditional pejorative meaning and dictionary definition – for certain character disorders in which the dynamics of hostility force a person to aberrant sexual acts. In other words, perversion implies an obligatory inclusion in the sexual act of defensive, alternate, or partial gratifications that allow genital release but usually not emotional intimacy. In contrast, 'deviation' implies a statistical abnormality; it describes an act not *usually* performed in certain circumstances within a given cultural milieu.

Devereux[5] emphasizes that from the intrapsychic point of view, the purpose of foreplay is to increase tension and to cathect the partner, whereas the purpose of perversion is to release tension and to decathect the partner; from the object relations point of view normal sexuality is characterized by true object cathexis in which the partner matters as an individual, is not used as a means to an end, is highly cathected, and is valued in the subject's and the partner's sexual gratification, whereas the so called passionate love relationships between perverts lack these characteristics. A pervert does not perceive the object of his love as a 'total' human being, but as a part object.

As Khan[6] has written, the pervert cannot surrender to his sexual experiences, but retains a split-off, dissociated, manipulative ego-control of the situation, which is both his achievement and failure in intimacy. It is this failure that supplies the compulsion to repeat the process. Although the pervert arranges and motivates the idealization of instinct which the technique of intimacy aims to fulfil, he himself remains outside the experiential climax. Hence, instead of instinctual gratification of object-cathexis, the pervert remains a deprived person whose only satisfaction has been of pleasurable discharge and intensified ego-interest.

Essential to the understanding of the complex psychopathology of these patients, are the elements of sadism, aggression and hostility. For example, Stoller[4] refers to "erotic hatred" and states that, "At the core of the perverse act is desire to harm others." Glasser[7] discusses the "Core complex", in which whenever such a person has the opportunity to be emotionally close to another person, he experiences a threat to his identity and withdraws. This leads to feelings of isolation and loneliness, which prompts longings for closeness, intertwined with which are intense aggressive feelings, over which he fears he will lose control. Another noteworthy characteristic is a strong, compelling, urge for immediate action; though the pervert knows that this action is wrong, he is unable to resist the impulse because it offers immediate relief from unbearable anxiety. Such heightened drive intensity is often based on childhood sexual traumata such as seduction and deprivation singly or in combination.[4]

In brief, most of our patients have deeply disturbed backgrounds. Some have criminal records and very low self-esteem which is often covered by a facade of cockiness and arrogance; their impulse control is minimal and they are suspicious and hateful towards people in authority. Some rebellious and violent ex-convicts have long histories of crime against property and persons. Others who feel insecure, inadequate and ashamed tend to be self-referrals. They enact their pathlogical sexual deviancy, such as exhibitionism, paedophilia or voyeurism, in a very secretive manner so that only their victims know about their behaviour. Some patients have a great capacity for expressing anger, yet seem shy and awkward in showing tenderness or love to anybody.

Patients are referred to us by various sources, such as mental hospitals, local GPs, probation officers, courts and other institutions. In some cases the public knowledge of a patient's sexual and/or criminal offence is very wide, as a result of the person having appeared in Court with associated press reports. At other times only patients themselves know about their 'bizarre' sexual behaviour and come to the Clinic of their own free will. All share an intense sense of shame and despondency about the activities in which they are involved. This is reciprocated by society's response to judge and condemn them when their behaviour is detected.

I am not sure that I can convey the amount of fear, rejection and humiliation which our patients experience when confronted with their 'secrets' in a conversation. This fear is greatly multiplied when they face not just one person but a group of let's say six or eight people for the first time. Of course, as complete strangers they are liable to project into the other members of the group their own sense of rejection and fear of being found unacceptable.

Clearly such patients present great difficulties for group analytic psychotherapy. Yet, they present a worthwhile challenge, when the potential benefits of a group experience for such 'anti-social' and 'asocial' people are considered. In the early days I almost gave up hope, because so many patients did not return after their first session. I was forced to think again about my whole approach.

It was vital to look more closely at particular psychopathologies and needs, and to see if the selection criteria could be improved. For example, given that such people present serious personality disorders and are unable to form relationships, it was obvious that some were more more suitable than others for group treatment. I became aware of the importance of certain factors in their personalities, family structure and living circumstances. For instance, the root family influence was crucial. Patients who had been subjected to an intense, suffocating relationship with one parent would be suitable candidates for group therapy. Groups provided them with a much warmer and less threatening atmosphere than they could usually find in one-to-one therapy, in which their experience of authority would be so intense. Also they could have a shared experience with their peers.

Often these people would still be subjugated to an over-possessive mother, who did not allow them to develop any independence or individuation. Others would leave home only to find themselves extremely isolated. In the group, with the help of fellow patients, they begin to express openly some rebellious, anti-authority feelings and eventually some self-assertion.

On the other hand, patients who had never experienced satisfactory relationships in early life are likely to do better in individual treatment, for example, those who came from very large families with financial deprivation and emotional overcrowding. However, patients who were adopted or fostered out, reacted in quite a different fashion when they joined a new group in which all members were "born" simultaneously, rather than one with previous history and traditions, in which they would feel "on trial" and closely observed by others, who were perceived as 'the old', 'legitimate', 'real' children (Of course, this is different when they are the original members and new ones are being incorporated into 'their' group).

I noticed that patients who had been evacuated to different homes during the war tended to react with terrifying fears of rejection and despondency when they joined an already established group.

A further problem arose from the patients' present living circumstances. There were those who could benefit from group therapy but were involved in the criminal world, should they open up and talk of their own or their spouse's criminal activities, the confidentiality rule would be impossible to sustain.

Violent behaviour seemed better contained and even better understood within the gramework of group therapy. Freud[8] points out that the mechanism of identification is a basic one in group formation, and he elaborates that identification not only helps to further positive feelings within the group, but also helps in limiting aggressiveness— since there is a general tendency to spare those with whom one is identified. The presence of other participants, who could notice hostility before it was expressed openly (often against the therapist), gave the group a capacity to confront violent behaviour and to deal with it openly and honestly. Multiple transferences provide patients with the possibility of more than just one target (as in one-to-one therapy), for their anger, which they found highly reassuring.

In contrast, extreme secretiveness was sometimes a contraindication. For example, John who came to the Clinic because of frotteurism, was a shy, awkward married man with children who had never confessed to anyone about this perversion, and even refused to give his address. At the first session, when he admitted to his problem, peoples' reaction seemed one of anxiety, covered by laughter. Everyone tried to minimize his symptom to such an extent that he felt humiliated, whereupon he became very flushed and left, never to return.

Sometimes patients presented themselves as 'perfect', 'ideal' patients for group therapy, but it transpired that they were rather good actors, often having been exposed previously to similar experiences in therapeutic prisons, or communities. Indeed, they became good helpers but got little for themselves. This did not mean that they should not be treated in groups, but that they warranted special consideration and might be treated more effectively in one-to-one psychotherapy.

I became aware of the importance of a thorough study of the composition of each particular group, using Foulkes'[3] description of the heterogeneous group as a "mixed bag of diagnoses and disturbances which are blended together to make a well balanced and therapeutically effective mixture . . . the greater the 'span' between the 'polar' types, the higher the therapeutic potential, if the group can stand it."

Pichon Riviere[9] too, said that the more heterogeneous the group, the more therapeutic it becomes.

Ideally the group should contain equal numbers of each sex, but in practice this proved to be difficult, since, women were referred much less often than men to the Clinic. On the other hand, I was able to mix patients who had sexual perversions with those who suffered form social deviancy or criminal behaviour. Similarly, it was necessary to consider how many homosexual men a group could contain, or how many heterosexual and homosexual paedophiliacs could be mixed in a group; likewise, how victims of incest were going to react to people who had committed incest with their own children. I learned that there was no particular law about these matters, but that it was best to err on the side of caution.

I discerned that I could minimize early drop outs by preparing patients prior to starting their treatment. Once a patient had been selected for a group, and a vacancy became available, he was given a number of irregular, brief individual interviews with his therapist. These promoted bonding between him and the therapist, as well as to the Clinic. The therapist confined him or herself to giving information about group rules, and encouraged the patient to pursue therapy despite the likelihood that he would want to leave the group after the first few sessions. The patient was informed that quite early on he could expect to develop a sense of belonging to the group. He was not encouraged to talk about himself in case rapport became too intense. The patient was given facts such as place, time and day of meetings of that particular group. I stressed the nature of the commitment and that it would go on for at least two years before it would be beneficial. I emphasized the importance of regularity and punctuality and that no group session would take place unless there were at least three members present on time.

If circumstances made his attendance impossible, he should let us know beforehand, because absenteeism created disturbances in the group. He was informed that after six consecutive missed sessions without prior notice he would be discharged, and that his place would be offered to another patient from the waiting list. In other words, commitment and responsibility towards themselves and the group were fundamental. This provided patients with a sense of continuity for which they were responsible.

Two other issues which I found important to emphasize were that of keeping material confidential to the group, and avoiding meeting with other members outside the group, since to do otherwise could easily jeopardize the treatment. They knew beforehand that once group therapy started no more individual interviews would be given to members of the group, so that all new and old conflicts would have to be dealt with entirely within the group. This also applied to requests for information from the outside, such as from GPs or probation officers. All members were expected to express their opinions and to give some consideration to the progress and changes happening to the particular patient about whom information had been requested. In case of relapse which might result in a member's court appearance (which often happened either at the beginning of therapy or when confronted with holidays) a colleague of mine would be responsible for the preparation of the new court report requested. This avoided acting out behaviour in which patients might feel themselves to be a 'favourite' or 'special' with their group conductor.

Some may say that to give all these regulations to people who have such strong tendencies for acting out could constitute a challenge and provocation, which they might meet by breaking the rules. Nevertheless, I considered that it was important to make the limits clear. At least they wouldn't be able to say later on, with a facade of innocence, "Oh well, we did not know about it." There would always be time to work through their acting out propensities and the expression of their anti-authority, rebellious feelings while in treatment.

Since using this preparation period, patients have been far more consistent in their attendance and the number of casualties has diminished to a minimum. If patients decided to leave their group they could get in touch with the Clinic again, instead of hiding away forever as they used to do.

Originally, I used a technique which closely followed Bion's idea of a work group, in other words I gave group interpretations of the here and now dynamics as the instrument of therapy and learning. I was aware of the basic assumption activity 'dependency', 'pairing', 'fight and flight'. However, slowly but steadily I began to change my approach, considering the particular psychopathology of each patient. I realized that a technique which provided these patients only with group interpretations seemed to reinforce their feelings of dehumanization and alienation, increasing their insecurity and lowering their self-esteem even more. In some cases, confusion and anxiety about their own identities were so intense that they were forced to leave the group quite suddenly.

It was not unusual, in the first group session, for them to cluster themselves, forming subgroups in order to avoid the fear of becoming individuals who would be liable to be rejected or not understood. For example, during one session people were saying that I devoted Mondays to shoplifters and homosexuals, Tuesdays to psychopaths, Wednesdays to child molesters and burglars etc. etc. In so doing perhaps they were hoping – dreading – that I could see them all as sub-group types without 'individual' characteristics. They were forcing on me a rôle like that of the head of a penal institution where inmates are depersonalized by numbers and criminal classification. This defensive attitude against being seen individually in the group was fostered by giving group interpretations at a transferential level. In so doing I would be colluding with their particular psycho-pathology.

It occurred to me that it would be far more efficacious after giving a group interpretation to link this with individual patient characterizations or pathologies. Thus, I was able to learn from Foulkes[10] more liberal use of the group situation, from his profound respect for the interpretations which might emanate from other members of the group, and from his belief that such comments could be more effective than those of the therapist. I also found useful his remarks about the therapist's attitude, "If the therapist has overcome in himself the claim to perfection, he is not afraid to be found wanting, imperfect and ignorant, he can allow himself to be honest and sincere and stand firm on the grounds of reality. In doing so he exerts by his own example, the most valuable and potent therapeutic influence." I was also influenced by his ideas that it is mistaken to think that the therapist is passive when he keeps himself in the background; actually while being receptive, he can be very active in his own mind, listening, devoting himself to understand what the group is saying or trying to say, very much engaged as to his own interventions. This model helps patients in their process of thinking as opposed to acting. Some identification of group members with their therapist takes place and they learn to wait patiently for the right time to intervene rather than make impulsive and useless gestures. I saw the need to become more firm and rigorous with these patients at times. I learned from Maxwell Jones how to allow active confrontation not only amongst members but occasionally between them and myself when I felt they needed firm leadership to relieve their own anxieties about ineffectual, uncaring parental figures. If the therapist took a 'democratic' attitude, it was experienced by our patients as a seductive manoeuvre. If, on the other hand, the leadership, was authoritarian their persecutory anxieties were reinforced. Both styles deprived patients of a real sense of boundary, and provided them with seduction during therapy and deprivation during holidays, thus recreating their disturbing familial pattern.

Of interest is that my style of conducting would change. Group members made perceptive remarks about this – to the effect that, if they were expected to change, why shouldn't the therapist change too. They noticed my adaptation to their needs rather than clinging to a technique which might provide me with a sense of security but would have left them feeling insecure and anonymous. I began to blend different techniques, according to the needs of each patient and what I thought was best for all.

I try to be consistent with regard to the interpretation of negative transferences. I interpret the negative transference from the very beginning of the group, since I believe this is the only effective way to deal with "unhealthy solidarity" and with all attempts to resist the development of group cohesion. Whenever patients get extremely angry with each other I include in the interpretation the quality of care which is present in this emotional response – in other words, that anger may convey concern.

The technique of discussing group interactions in great detail I found to be of great importance for the development of positive therapeutic insight but also would enable them to think about their actions and to take responsibility for the life of the group and its survival. This is essential for a person who is prone to acting out behaviour to relieve mounting anxiety at times of distress. We see our patients only once a week and they are without any support until they come the following week. They seem very vulnerable to mishaps, especially during holidays when they miss the group attendances and feel themselves rejected. A missed session may provoke a member to embark on all sorts of delinquent activity. It is perhaps a month later, after repeated interpretations and working through that it starts to click with him that there is a link between such activity and missing a session.

At the Portman Clinic we never use such auxiliary devices as the one way screen, video recording etc. We are aware that we are missing something of value for training and teaching purposes, but we consider that our first priority is the sense of well-being of our patients. They have already experienced rejection, humiliation and isolation and might find unacceptable any devices which increase a sense of distrust and fears of being persecuted or blackmailed. This also applies to the use of a co-therapist or observers in a group, which I feel strongly could hamper their reliance on the group and the therapist. I suspect that to confront them with a couple of therapists would evoke in them primal scene fantasies, and would be even more likely to trigger off violent attacks, especially on holidays when they might feel deserted by "parents" who go away together. When only one therapist is present and the patients confront her, the facts suggest that she is a bit like the "have-nots": she is in authority, she determines the holidays, she is the so-called 'normal' one, but still she is alone, and, therefore, she is seen as understanding trust.

On arrival patients go to a waiting room adjacent to the receptionist's area. Exactly at the time for the session patients are invited to go to the group therapy room downstairs, where the therapist is waiting for them. Chairs are arranged in circular fashion and a sheet of paper with blank spaces and dates of sessions is on a table. Members write their own names in the first session and tick their attendance in the corresponding blank date. This procedure was adopted after careful study of the circumstances involved. Had their names and surnames already been typed down before the meeting it might be thought to denote a faulty sense of confidentiality, hence we leave it open for them to write whatever name they want to be identified with. Not only is it useful for me to have a record of their attendance, but it also increases their sense of commitment and responsibility towards the group. It also creates a fixed sense of belonging and a sense of care for those absent.

As soon as they begin to express concern for those absent, it becomes part of the philosophy of treatment for them to write letters to those absent patients which the Clinic forwards (keeping addresses completely confidential). It is most rewarding to see patients composing letters, from the moment in which one of them is selected or volunteers to do so, so much is involved in this process of identification. Different members dictate sentences which are taken or rejected until eventually the letter is ready. Our groups are slow open and we introduce new patients perhaps twice a year. This requires long term work prior to their arrival. Sometimes they will welcome the idea of new arrivals in a most emphatic manner. They talk of "new blood" being injected into the group, and express all sorts of fantasies of new members who will be suitable matches for them. It is not unusual at these times for patients to make references to having placed advertisements in "lonely columns" of different magazines. At other times an atmosphere of conning develops and intense fear is created by the thought of new members coming.

The first session of a newly established group

The first group session is of vital importance for the understanding of the psychopathologies of these individuals who tend to react in a similar manner. Unlike a group of neurotic patients, when they first confront each other, there won't be many sticky silences. On the contrary, once somebody starts talking everybody joins in and the whole atmosphere is enlivened: often there will be almost simultaneous presentation of two themes. One of minimizing symptoms and seeing themselves as misunderstood victims of society — it will be implied that on the whole they are good, caring citizens, who feel trapped in all the misunderstandings that surround them. The other is of being victims of intense persecution. Immediately an authority figure will emerge, usually a policeman who is just there to humiliate, persecute, blackmail or torture them. There is oscillation between these ways of dealing with their predicament.

It is not unusual for members to conjure up an image of a "nagging" or possessive mother of whom they have been both frightened and rather contemptuous. They will tend to agree with each other, thus creating an atmosphere of unhealthy solidarity with the main object of assigning that image to the therapist. They will try in very devious ways to get the therapist to collude with their perversions, involving her in such a way that, unless transferential interpretations are made very early, the therapeutic process will become extremely difficult to handle. The therapist may be trapped with few options, such as becoming the sadistic policeman who every time they talk about their problems will try to moralize, condemn, or put them away, or a nagging mother who invariably will use the group to question every patient in a persistent and repetitive way about their illegal activities, expecting them to conform to society's norms. Patients will display extraordinary cunning in the presentation of their problems, and the other members will react to create a 'grand confession'. Unhealthy solidarity often appears to condone members' criminal actions. With the utmost fear of pseudo acceptance, they will try to put all the 'blame' outside in society.

Projective mechanisms are well in play in these groups. A patient in his first session said that his main problem was an intense urge to steal female underwear from clothes lines, to take home to masturbate with. Anxiety generated in the group was quite formidable, until another member (in this case a female patient who had a background of extremely violent behaviour) became extremely kind and understanding (a 'bad' understanding). She told him, "Well I don't think that is such a serious problem. After all, it involves only the theft of a pair of knickers, which would cost about 50p. So, in other words, you appeared in court for the theft of 50p." She was trying to relieve the patient's anxiety about the action but was doing absolutely nothing to assist with understanding the motivations of the patient.

Again, a heterosexual paedophiliac who had just been caught molesting and seducing a young girl of 6, presented his case in very indignant terms and talked about the harmful effect which the police action had on the child and the child's family because of their brusque intervention in the case. The police were the ones who had created the problem; had interfered with that child's normal development and were causing them all a terrible trauma with irreversible effects on the child and family. Other patients tend to sympathize, again omitting any consideration of the patient's motivations for his own action.

An important theme which appears in the course of therapy

It is remarkable how quickly patients develop a sense of belonging. Symbolically speaking, it is as though the group stands for an ever available breast to satisfy their longings to be fed on demand. Although eventually they come to terms with the once-a-week rhythm, holidays are distressing for them. During breaks they feel neglected and abandoned; they miss the group so much and tend to get involved in dangerous acting out. One aspect of this clinical problem is their tendency to criticise and debase the group process. Case examples will serve to illustrate both the therapeutic opportunity as well as the risks surrounding holiday breaks.

Paul had referred himself for treatment because of heterosexual paedophilia — from the start he created a strong dependence on me as he had with his mother. To use symbolism descriptively again I thought that he wished to be fed on demand by an ever-available breast represented by the group. The dates for the first summer holiday break were announced almost two months in advance. Everyone had been informed at the outset about official holidays. Despite this Paul was shocked; he had assumed that I was accessible at all times and was living in at the Clinic. A good deal of interpretive work was done about separation anxieties, but it was disconcertingly clear that Paul was unable to accept the reality of the forthcoming holiday. He began to behave like a deserted child. For the first time he talked in detail of what exactly took place between him and the little girls involved in his actions. He did 'warn' us that he had disgusted his father in Court by telling how he pursued the girls in the playground. I noticed that the whole group became mesmerized by this account. There were no interruptions, no confrontations, no questioning. There was not only silence, but the whole atmosphere was charged; everybody was excited and sexually aroused. This patient had succeeded in turning the whole group into a child and he was the molester. He was deriving pleasure for himself in this situation and no longer needed to seduce children outside in the 'Playground'. In the group he was unconsciously displaying his perversion and others in the group were responding as though they were the child described by him who obtains sexual gratification with full consent.

Apparently he did not force, but rather seduced the child.

As if to subdue their intense oral needs and subsequent depression, the group begins to interact with one of its members in a rather manic fashion, listening to his erotic talk about sexually perverse material (this would seem to involve an oedipal phenomenon but actually corresponds to earlier phases of development: physical closeness is the common theme). The patient goes on talking about his sexual predicament with extreme richness of detail. This might denote great trust in the group on his part, but the fact that a particular patient talked with such freedom and so openly about actions when previously he seemed so ashamed, should make the therapist suspicious. It soon becomes obvious that the patient is using the group session itself, relating to the group as a whole as to a partner for his perversion. In other words, by describing with such richness his criminal and sexual offences, the patient is trying to seduce and excite other members, thereby getting enormous sexual gratification. The time and place for therapy become the time and place for perversion instead. Sometimes the talk might be about such weekly expeditions to shoplift or to 'cottage' the lavatories seeking homosexual experiences. That particular group member would be using the weekly session, to coin a symbol, as a lavatory to be rid of all the dirt inside. In colluding with this the group takes on a cathartic purpose, and not a therapeutic one. On all these occasions a climate of intense excitement is created by the very richness of material proffered. At other times a violent threat is cast upon the group by an angry member. This causes fear mixed with excitement, which our patients are so vulnerable too. The patient may not act out in his social context, but he does within the group through the way he talks and interacts with the group as a whole. The latter can be analyzed unlike the former.

Susan is yet another example of this phenomenon. A stripteaser-prostitute, she revealed very little of herself in the first few sessions. After a few months, just before the Easter holidays, in a slow and determined fashion, she began to show bits of herself in a provocative and seductive manner, e.g. her difficulties in having a one-to-one relationship, her contempt of men not being as competent or capable as she was expecting them to be, her fears of commitment, her close association with her daughter aged nine, her sense of boredom, her skill in mastering men, and eventually in a most histrionic manner she talked about the way she seduced men for financial profit. By then the group was behaving like a dirty old man, unable to question or to confront her but only too willing to give her all the attention and whatever she wanted out of the situation. These examples show a repetitive pattern of behaviour which engulfs the group in a status quo.

The conductor tries to be skilful in dealing with such interactions from the outset. Failing to interpret during a session may result in the arrest of therapeutic development. Collusion for comfort makes interpretation leading to insight unlikely. This same collusion associated with an intense fear of criticism arising from discussion of motivations therefore operates to spare patients and therapist supposed condemnation. In consequence though, all this will create another anxiety because members are aware that covering up brings frustrations when the conductor doesn't intervene properly by offering adequate interpretations. Unless unhealthy expectations can be interpreted quickly, the therapist and his expertise are likely to be immobilised.

In my view when working with criminals and deviants the therapeutic task is to facilitate a movement towards acting less and suffering more, whereas with neurotics, it is to help them to suffer less and to act more.

I would like to emphasize how rewarding my experiences with such patients has been. Although they offer a great challenge, they cherish their opportunity for therapy and it is gratifying to see how much they can change.

References

1. Bion, W.R. Experiences in groups, and other papers. Tavistock Publications, 1968.
2. Jones, Maxwell *et al.* Social Psychiatry: A Study of Therapeutic Communities. Tavistock Publications: 1952.
   Jones, Maxwell. Beyond the Therapeutic Community. New Haven, Yale University Press: 1968.
3. Foulkes, S.H. Introduction to Group Analytic Psychotherapy. Heinemann Medical Books 1948.
   Therapeutic Group Analysis. London. Allen & Unwin 1964.
   Group Analytic Psychotherapy, Method and Principles. London Gordon & Breach: 1975.
4. Stoller, R.J. Perversion: the erotic form of hatred: Harvester Press, 1976.
5. Devereux, G. Scientific Proceedings Midwinter Meeting, 1953. Panel Report 3 – Perversion: Theoretical and Therapeutic Aspects. Journal Am. Psycho-analytic Assoc. 1954 Vol. 2 p. 336-345.
6. Khan, M. "The function of intimacy and acting out in perversion" from "Sexual behaviour and the Law" ed. R. Slovenko. Springfield, Illinois; Charles C. Thomas 1965 p. 402.
7. Glasser, M. "The core complex" in a chapter "Some aspects of the role of aggression in the perversions" from Sexual Deviations" ed. by I. Rosen. Oxford University Press 1979.
8. Freud, S. Group Psychology and the Analysis of the Ego. Hogarth Press, London 1959.
9. Pichon Riviere, Personal Communication 1961.
10. Foulkes, S.H. "A Memorandum on Group Therapy: British Military Memorandum ADM 11 BM (mimeographed) July 1945.

The Group-Analytic Treatment of Drinking Problems

By FERNANDO ARROYAVE

Introduction

Alcoholism and alcohol-related problems represent today an increasing part of medical practice. A considerable percentage of *all* admissions to both General and Psychiatric Hospital are the result of alcohol abuse. Yet, despite this fact, health workers show insufficient interest in the identification and treatment of such disabilities in my view.

Alcoholism is a very complex entity. The interaction between personality, social factors, psychodynamic causation and possibly genetic influence makes up such complexity. In this chapter I shall deal exclusively with the rôle of Group Analytic Psychotherapy in the treatment of alcohol-related problems and shall assume that the reader is familiar with concepts of definition, identification and other treatment aspects of alcoholism.

Group Analysis is *not* the only method to treat these problems and there is reasonable evidence to suggest that a good number of problem drinkers need exposure to a variety of methods before they engage themselves in the process of *change,* without which success is unlikely and relapses are very common.

My interest in this area of practice goes back 15 years and the ideas here described are the result of my work at the Oxford Region Alcoholism Unit where well over 4,000 patients have been treated over the past 12 years.

Basic Principles

I refer the reader to chapters where principles of group analysis as first postulated by Foulkes have been described in detail. I shall limit myself to outline areas and points of special relevance to the group analysis of alcoholics.

But before this, it is important to establish the difference between group-analysis and group psychotherapy. The former means the resolution of any thing complex into its simple elements. This is carried out in a group situation governed and guided by principles referred to elsewhere in this book. The final result aims to understand complex behaviour and to modify it as much as possible. Group-analysis does not mean that a cure, in the strict medical sense, will follow, nor that behaviour must change totally and fundamentally.

Psychotherapy, on the other hand, is a method of treatment in which a therapist deliberately establishes a relationship with a patient with the object of removing symptoms and/or a disturbed pattern of behaviour. Psychotherapy may be formal or informal, depending on whether the person has received special professional training. Group analysis implies, by definition, that the conductor has received special training and does his work within a theoretical framework.

The setting should be always the same in relation to room, chairs, general furnishings, pictures etc., so as to ensure that all material comes from the internal worlds of the patients and is not related in any possible way to real changes in their environment.

The contract must be the same for all patients and all should receive the information in the same manner.

The conductor should refrain from having any contact with his patients other than within the group and its administration, and should specially be careful in *not* prescribing drugs. If this is necessary an outside physician should be responsible for it.

Alcohol is a powerful drug. Its ingestion alters not only behaviour, but affects insight, emotions and judgement, and does so even in small quantities. Abstinence, is therefore, an absolute *must* for the successful treatment of drinking problems. It is clear from this, that abstinence is a prerequisite for treatment and not the result of it.

Alcohol as a theme in the group must be interpreted as soon as possible thus taking the group rapidly to a different level of working, preferably to the interaction and significance between dependence and relationships.

The unconscious communication that takes place in a group of alcoholics is particularly strong and because of this, any subject raised or comment made by any member of the the group can and should be heard as the very strong voice of the group.

Many alcoholics do have great difficulty in verbally expressing their feelings. Special attention must be paid here to the silent and non-verbal communciation of the group.

Interpretations ideally should come from the group members and the work of the conductor directed to clarify, enlarge and guide in such a way as to make the group able to understand their behaviour and interpret it in simple, everyday language.

The use of "deep" interpretations, especially those touching areas related to Oedipal experience and homosexuality should be avoided and only reached after lengthy and careful "working-through". To forget this, can result in disaster and trigger-off acting-out behaviour and drinking "binges" with calamitous consequences.

It is better not to single out individuals within the group and in those cases where the conductor finds it appropriate, such work should always be interlinked with the group as a whole or at least with two or three individuals using relevant material so as to help contain strong paranoic tendencies often exhibited by alcoholics.

The frequency, regularity and total length (in time) of groups depend on the circumstances. In residential situations (hospital in-patient treatment) treatment can be as intense as two groups daily for a period of three weeks. In the long-term, frequency should be not less than once a week and ideally twice a week.

I have found that whatever the length (three weeks or three years) the experience of starting and finishing a group together is important for individuals, who, almost without exception, have deep-seated problems of separation anxiety and sibling rivalry.

Patients need individual attention as well as the group experience and this may lead to practical problems though there is no objection to it, providing that *all members* of the group are aware that individual sessions are available to anyone if and when needed.

Selection of patients for Group Analysis

The field of selection of patients for psychotherapy is full of myths and misconceptions, most of which are based on the writings of the early pioneers of psychoanalysis and psychotherapy. Group analysis being a relatively recent method had no time to look in detail at all parameters, and the review of literature shows little about selection of patients with drinking problems for group-analysis.

I am not aware of any published work, by group-analysts, related to the treatment of such patients. The writings of psychoanalysts and psychotherapists of all creeds too, have hardly matched the prominence of drink problems. This is to be regretted but in my view the group analytic method offers the best choice for the large majority of alcoholics and opens up great therapeutic possibilities.

My criteria for selecting patients have changed progressively, and widened more over the years.

Number

The number with which I work in an analytic group ranges from six to eight and is a somewhat personal matter. Having observed a large number of conductors I am well aware that each one has a number of people that he feels comfortable to work with. My own preferred number is seven or eight (plus myself) and ideally the distribution of sexes should be roughly equal.

Age

Most of my work takes place in the setting of the National Health Service. This means that selection of patients is almost impossible as I have a statutory duty to provide a service for *all* individuals with alcohol problems. It can be easily understood then that my criteria for selecting patients are rather broad and I must find strong "good" reasons to justify the exclusion of patients.

This applies to all variables such as age, social class, status, intelligence etc. In relation to age I have successfully mixed ages, including large discrepancies, although in doing so care has to be exercised to avoid isolates of extreme ages by ensuring that there is always someone of similar age and preferably of the same sex with whom each can identify. The myth that the age 40 is the limit over which patients should be excluded certainly does not apply to alcoholics and, to the contrary, I have found that patients between 40 and 55 respond better than those younger or older.

Other parameters

With regard to social status and cultural background I have found that the greater the mixture, the better the process develops. One has to look at the group as an experimental reproduction of life experience and in my experience, mixing individuals of different social status and background provides an excellent opportunity for learning. It should be noted, however, that such mixtures demand a conductor not only technically skilled but experienced in matters of life.

An exception to this rule is that of mixing the so called "school of vagrants" with other social categories of patients. The "culture" of these vagrants is so powerful that it influences the group, to its detriment. I have witnessed, almost with disbelief, the sudden and dramatic change that a small subgroup of vagrants effects on a group. If one wants to treat vagrants in a group they must be "diluted" and no more than two of them (no less either) should participate. This category of patients presents special problems and they often need more structured and disciplined techniques. To work with these patients one needs to be constantly aware of countertransference feelings and regular supervision is a "sine qua non" for the process of treatment to evolve successfully.

It has often been said that in order to profit from psychotherapy or analysis individuals need to have a high I.Q. At the very beginning of my work with alcoholics I fell foul of such popular belief but this, among other "dogmas", was irreversibly broken down by the light of experience. It is true that the type of defences, as well as the manner in which individuals use them varies according to intelligenge (among parameters) but normal I.Q. or indeed slightly below normal is not an impediment for anyone to profit from the experience of psychotherapy. As with many other variables mixing individuals with different degrees of intellectual ability favours and fosters the necessary interaction for good learning. Once more here I must emphasize the rôle of the conductor in keeping the "necessary balance" in the group and ensuring that defences such as rationalization and intellectualization are not abused. He should be well aware of the need to maximize simple language and discourage the use of jargon. Rarely do I exclude a patient on such grounds and if so, only on the basis of a very low I.Q. bordering on subnormality. Very often I have found that placing patients with just normal range of intelligence among more fortunate and articulate individuals forces the latter to "descend from the clouds" and to find simple, everyday language which is better for learning and good communication.

Patients with "special problems" like homosexuality, sexual deviations, physical deformities and extreme introversion should, if possible, have a person with similar problems within the group to facilitate identification and to mirror their progress through it. The difficulty of dealing with such problems has been greatly exaggerated. I would mention especially patients who have great difficulties in verbalizing and expressing feelings and ideas. Alcoholics often have such problems and they may be excluded from therapeutic groups on this basis. I know of no reasonable explanation to adopt such a policy. This category of patients is capable (like most others) of working and benefiting from groups. The conductor can keep in mind the fact that the ability to verbalize and the number and length of interventions are not necessarily related to outcome and that a good part of the group process occurs at an unconscious leve. Exclusion of patients with this disadvantage may be related to countertransference difficulties of the conductor who constantly needs the reassurance of patients and feels persecuted by their silence. It would be a pity to exclude anyone from a group who shows such reticence.

There is only one category of patients that should, in my view, be excluded from group analytic therapy, and then only temporarily. I refer to those individuals who exhibit extreme anxiety and who tend, as a result, to act out. This subgroup of patients should have special preparation. The manner in which I get them "ready" is by encouraging a strong transference in the course of three to five individual sessions. It is important that this is done by the group-analyst who is going to conduct the group later on, since the presence of another therapist may precipitate a great deal of disappointment which can be acted out. In most cases I have not used medication of any kind to lower their anxiety and when I have done this it has not been difficult for me to recognize later on, that I have been trapped by my own feelings, about keeping a patient suffering unnecessarily.

There is one final category of patients which I want to consider in terms of selection. They are well known and anyone who treats alcoholics comes across them only too often. They are those individuals who are without insight and motivation, who *do not* want to stop drinking and who, furthermore, think that they can handle alcohol perfectly well. They usually come to treatment because of strong external pressures and complying with it is one of their ways of carrying on in the same way. These patients are extremely difficult to treat, often drop out in the middle of treatment and can be very disruptive for the group as a whole. Despite all these considerations I have no hesitation in including them for group analysis. Sometimes their defences can be modified and then they make an excellent response to analysis.

What is relevant here is that there is no reliable method to predict outcome and therefore any reasonable and trained group analyst has, in my view, (and specially trained within the N.H.S. setting) the moral obligation to accept for therapy as many alcoholics as possible.

Each therapist has his own personal limitations and, as a general rule, if one feels that working with a particular patient is going to be particularly cumbersome it is best not to try. The group analyst has a special responsibility to reduce his "blind spots" but patients who provoke serious doubts about therapist competence should be offered treatment by a senior and more experienced group analyst.

Finally a few words about violent patients. Obviously inclusion of such individuals in analytic groups must be related to how far a clinical therapeutic team think and feel that they can manage problems arising. Circumstances such as limited medical cover at night, pregnant women on the staff, condition of the building and ratio between staff and patient come into consideration. My own practice is to discuss such patients openly and in detail at a clinical meeting and to accept them *only* if there is good staff agreement. It is hardly necessary to make the point that ability to contain and deal with violent patients is directly related to awareness and sophistication of the therapeutic team.

Reviewing our experience over many years I feel more inclined to include patients in groups and that a sensible rule is to approach the process of selection inversely, i.e. that compelling reasons must be found to exclude a person.

Patients should always be seen by the conductor of the group and if possible on more than one occasion. The only exception to this golden rule is in a residential situation where the patient comes to be treated by a therapeutic team, and where group analysis is only *part* (however important) of the whole process.

Contracts

Therapeutic contracts are fashionable these days and much has been said and written about them. I like to look at contracts in terms of parameters which may help the individuals to profit from the experience that they are about to enter into.

Prior information can be standardized so that all receive the same briefing. First of all patients are given all pertinent details of likely duration, starting date, timetable and all relevant information about the setting in which treatment is to take place (residential, out-patients, private etc.).

Secondly the contract proper should be established. This includes:

(1) A personal commitment to sobriety either during the period of admission (if groups are to take place in a residential setting) or while attending the groups. (if the groups take place on an out-patient basis).

(2) A personal commitment to avoid drugs other than those prescribed by a qualified doctor.

(3) The commitment to attend the group for the whole of the time (in the case of short-term groups up to one month) and to give reasonable notice otherwise (at least three months).

Goals

Treatment involves many complex issues. When talking about treatment a possible outcome of normal drinking may arise.

This is not possible, in my view, and would imply a collusion with the pseudo-delusional system of the alcoholic. Furthermore a large number of alcoholics who enter into group analytic treatment do have long-standing personality problems which even with treatment often do not clear completely and require a long process of analysis. The group analyst must become well aware of the likely possibility that the patient may be using the abstinence issue to enact a struggle like that of his early relationship with parental figures. The liability of "being made" into an omnipotent, overprotective mother is not to be taken lightly.

Pain and a certain amount of suffering are good signs in the process of change and therapists, particularly if medically qualified, should not go out of their way to protect "their children".

It follows that the question of goals must be approached with great caution and in the short term only three are realistic and achievable. They are as follows:

(1) The conviction that lifelong sobriety is a necessary requirement for any constructive personality changes to take place.

(2) The full and positive internal acceptance that each individual is responsible for his own actions and that external circumstances cannot be used as an excuse for individual behaviour.

(3) The realization that personal changes involve long and laborious processes for which the individual has responsibility, though often help is needed to proceed with them.

I am of the opinion that any other goals are superfluous and often unrealistic; for the alcoholic who has been drinking for many years, seems incapable of deciding what he really wants.

The Rôle of the conductor

The Conductor has special responsibility for creating a culture where effective communication in the group develops smoothly. Many patients with drinking problems share the difficulty of expressing themselves properly, and this, combined with a low tolerance to frustration present the conductor with the particular problem of how to create an environment where individuals "can take the risk" of participating verbally. This question of stress tolerance is not confined to groups for alcoholics but the conductor in this special situation should participate more actively than he would in groups for neurotics to begin with, so ensuring that anxiety levels do not go beyond the limits that can be contained by the group.

Asking, clarifying, opening up ways of exploring any situation and doing so without interfering with the group processes is his main function in the early stages. He will pay special attention to the main defences exhibited by the alcoholic patient, namely, denial, rationalization and projection.

The avoidance of jargon is of the greatest importance and any attempts to introduce technical language should be seen as counterproductive.

The use of historical interpretations is not advisable but rather the analysis of behaviour can be encouraged by drawing attention to present interactions within the group.

Interventions by the conductor using parental relationships as an explanation for behaviour provokes strong resistances.

There is advantage in the conductor making his own position in relation to abstinence emphatically clear from the beginning, leaving the group in no doubt.

Analysts (both individual and group) are often reluctant to take firm stands and sometimes get carried away by their omnipotence in leading the alcoholic to believe that a return to normal drinking is possible and fall within therapeutic expectations. I have seen that the result of such a "technique" almost always had disastrous consequences.

It is important that group members end synchronously, regardless of duration. All alcoholics, without exception, have difficulties in dealing with separation and the ending of a group is, probably, the most important experience that they can have with the group. The learning possibilities of the ending are crucial and I am of the opinion that without "working through" this phase drinking relapses are almost the rule. For the group-analyst who works with alcoholic patients the termination involves him too with the separation process.

Health workers of all disciplines often hold distorted "beliefs" about individuals with drinking problems having a poor prognosis. Nothing could be further from what my practice taught me. These patients are as rewarding to work with as any other category. Perhaps it depends on how each group analyst responds to the challenge of dealing with so called "impossible problems" and whether he is prepared for a struggle to modify his method.

"A woman has two images. There is a magical person seen or remembered by those who love her, her finest qualities are flesh and spirit illuminated. She herself knows this ideal self; she projects it, if she is confident; or she day-dreams her ideal self; or she recognizes it with gratitude in the admiring eyes of others. There is at the same time a second image; the woman as seen by those who dislike or fear her. This cruel picture has an all too powerful mirror in her own negative idea of herself. She sees with fear her own ravaging impulses and most painful of all, a graceless, freakish, and unlovable physical self, this was the mirror her parents held before Edith. Her brothers saw her with love. She herself knew both images. Her life, and her poetry, constituted a flight from the second one."

From "Edith Sitwell. A Biography", by Victoria Glendinning. Weidenfeld and Nicholson, London 1981. p. 35.

Mirroring in Group Analysis as a Developmental and Therapeutic Process

By MALCOLM PINES

The information about mirroring is widely scattered and the search for it is rather like a treasure hunt, moving from clue to clue. I began with clinical observations in group analysis and psychoanalysis in the company of Foulkes,[1] Yalom,[2] Kohut[3] and Lacan;[4/5] moved to the literature on child development where, to my surprise Charles Darwin[6] was one of the first observers of a child's reaction to his mirror image; psychoanalysts who have made significant clinical contributions to the developmental aspects of mirroring include Winnicott,[7] Lichtenstein,[8] Mahler,[9] Shengold[10] and Bursten;[11] experimental observations on the child's development of self recognition have been made amongst others by Amsterdam,[12] Lewis and Brooks-Gunn,[13] based on Piaget's developmental stages and using techniques that originated in the investigations on primates to determine whether they have a self-image. What has been shown[14] is that chimpanzees, in contrast to all other animals, are able to use a mirror image to explore their own bodies from which we can confidently infer that they have a self schema based upon visual perception. At the human level Cooley described the "looking glass self",[15] that we constitute our images on the reflected appraisal of others and it is on this base that G.H. Mead[16] built his theory of symbolic interaction. The looking glass metaphor for the human mind, that we see by reflection and not by direct vision, is an ancient one that has dominated Western thought since Plato and in Eastern thought the mirror is one of the most sacred symbols of the Japanese Shinto religion.[17] So long did the looking glass metaphor dominate Western thought that only in the 18th century did our poetic literature change its metaphor for the mind from the mirror to the lamp;[18] with the rise of the Romantic movement and the privatization of inner space the mind of the poet was now likened to a lamp that illuminates the vast darkness of the human mind and soul in place of the mirror that can only reflect external reality. The mind as a mirror can easily falsify the truth and seduce us into illusion. Narcissus died because he could not free himself from the illusory world of images and enter into the world of object relations, the social world. The image of Narcissus and the mirror featured prominently in mediaeval literature, a literature which itself reflected the evolution of self consciousness and of individuality.[19] The tragedy of Narcissus, of man and womankind, was that even after Narcissus recognized that he was in love with his own reflection, he could not free himself from its spell. Thus the narcissistic mirror selectively only reflects the self and excludes the vision of the other.

Snow White's cruel stepmother was enraged when her mirror showed not her own face as the fairest of them all; the social mirror based on the reflected appraisals of others told the Ugly Duckling that he had indeed become a swan. The move from the narcissistic to the social mirror is reflected in George Herbert's phrase "the best mirror is a good friend".

The mind of Western man and the nature of his art forms are described, far more often than we realize, in terms of mirrors and of mirroring.[20] Though I shall soon turn to those aspects of mirroring that were first described by S.H. Foulkes in analytic group psychotherapy, the mutual mirroring and reflection that patients quickly engage in, I would like first to remind you of the richness of our language in mirror and ocular metaphors. The root of the word mirror is related to marvel, miracle and mirages, a rich triad of images. When we say that we see something we mean that we understand; when we are in ignorance and doubt we see as into a glass darkly. Ben Johnson praised Shakespeare for holding the mirror up to nature and Shakespeare's Elizabethan scientific contemporary Francis Bacon[21] said that "the mind of man is far from the nature of a clear and equal glass, wherein the beams of things should reflect according to their true incidence; nay, it is rather like an enchanted glass, full of superstitition and imposture if it be not reduced." When we try to look into ourselves, at our inner nature, we are engaged in self-reflection. Man looks for his soul by looking deeply into his mirror images directly or through the art forms. Stendhal in "The Red and the Black" wrote that "the novel is a mirror strolling down a broad highway. Sometimes it reflects the azure blue of the skies, sometimes the mire stagnating in the muddy ditches". The magic of the mirror, like the magic of the mind, is that a whole world can be encompassed in one single vision so that time and space, the enormous diversity of human experience can be seen within the boundaries and the structures of the mind.

The Romantic Movement of the 19th century was deeply absorbed in the imaginative exploration of the theme of the double, of shadow and the mirror image. These images of the unconscious were soon to be released from the realm of the imaginary into the discourse of psychological science by Freud and his colleagues amongst whom Rank[22] and Roheim[23] took a particular interest in mirrors and doubles.

Before turning back to group psychotherapy I would like to tell you a mirror story. In the Tsarist Russia a weary poor Jewish pedlar reached an inn where he hoped to stay the night. He was told that the only bed left was in a room already occupied by a general who was already asleep and he could sleep there only on the condition that he did not disturb the great man's sleep. So he quietly undressed in the dark and in the morning crept out quietly. On the staircase was a large mirror and as he descended in it he beheld a bemedalled and epauletted full Russian general. "My God" he cried "what a mistake they have made – they've woken the wrong man."

Mirroring in group psychotherapy can be considered as the impact of information about the self that is derived through social interaction and relationship in the setting of an analytic group. The structure of the group is the mirror's setting, its boundaries of time and space the mirror's frame. The backing, the opacity which transforms the sheet of glass into a reflective surface, is the analytic culture which steadily promotes reflection and understanding of unconscious processes. The mirroring process is the steady to and fro rhythm of externalization and internalization, me in you and you in me. It is only on the basis of communality that differences become meaningful as figure against ground. Just as apples and pears are not identical but are both fruits, so that patients in the group can establish valid differences on the basis of a firmly developed group matrix. These differences are established through the analysis of transference, lateral to the other group members, central to the group conductor and to the group entity itself. The transferences have to develop and to be recognized and analyzed. In the group analytic situation the analysis of transference is as much the prerogative and responsibility of the group members as it is of the conductor whose vision is largely centred on the group as a whole. It is the response of group members to transference projections that leads to recognition and working out of transference relationships and which enables further work to be done beyond transference, which is the deeper encounter and exploration of self and other against which transference is often a defence.

The group matrix, the foundation ground upon which the interpersonal and transpersonal processes of group analysis take place, is itself, I believe, based upon mirroring processes and upon resonance. Here I refer to the very earliest mirroring processes, the silent establishment of the mirroring frame of reference that Mahler describes which is based on the selective response by the "environmental mother", to use Winnicott's term, to the infant. Mother and child develop a way of being together which in good enough circumstances establishes an emotional field of forces from which the infant gradually differentiates as it acquires the capacity for autonomous existence in the process of separation-individuation. This early psychic matrix is laid down on the basis of reciprocity of gaze, sound and touch as much recent infant observation amply testifies.[24] There is a circularity of response between infant and mother from which develops the spiral of increasing differentiation. The mother encourages and leads the child upwards developmentally by giving meaning to its random actions. The child's smile or grasp is regarded by the mother as meaning that the child *intended* the gesture; "you are a clever boy to do that" in response to a baby's chance action that she, mother wants to see as representing the child's intention and his response to her. The mother insists on being recognized and that the baby recognize itself as the source of intentionality, of self.[25] The mother clothes her baby in conversational gestures from which develop the proto-conversation of mother and child.[26] The more the group members can see and feel their every experience to be meaningful to the group as a whole, so their basic matrix of self is remobilized and worked through in the new group field. At a deep level this remobilizes the laying down of the "coherent unconscious" that Loewald[27] differentiates from the "incoherent unconscious". The "coherent unconscious" of the healthy person is the foundation stone of integrity and creativity, whereas the "incoherent unconscious" is the source of disruptive emotional conflict.

Quite early in his observations of small groups conducted analytically, S.H. Foulkes noted what he came to call "mirror phenomena". His frame of reference was the group as a whole, in which every event even though apparently confined to one or two participants, in fact involves the group as a whole. He grouped together location, mirror reaction, occupation and translation as group specific phenomena.[28]

"Mirror reactions are characteristically brought out when a number of persons meet and interact. The person sees himself, or part of himself – often a repressed part of himself – reflected in the interactions of other group members. He sees them reacting in the way he does himself, or in contrast to his own behaviour. He also gets to know himself – and this is a fundamental process in ego development – by the effect he has on others and the picture they form of him." Elsewhere he describes the child's emergence from narcissism through the greater awareness of the self evoked by reflections coming from outside which help him differentiate between what he is and what he is not. As to the mechanisms of the mirror reaction he says that it "can be dissected into a number of psychoanalytic concepts e.g. projection, identification etc. but there are good grounds for putting these together and giving them a collective name emphasizing the 'mirror' aspect." Despite saying no more than this Foulkes undoubtedly considered mirroring to be a fundamental group analytic process and therapeutic mechanism. This is not a concept which he derived from psychoanalysts; note that he says that "mirror reactions are characteristically brought out when a *number* of persons meet and interact". It is based upon the observer position; "he can observe from the outside another member reacting in the way he, himself, reacts, can for instance see how conflicts and problems are translated into neurotic behaviour". Thus it was an observation sui generis, derived from the field of observation of the small group, the new therapeutic context that he had established. It is not simply a transference manifestation either on a parental or peer level; it was rather a concept based upon a self psychology of persons whose selves are incomplete, recognizing aspects of themselves "in particular a repressed part" in other persons. Foulkes noted that persons could often more easily recognize how conflicts and problems are translated into neurotic behaviour when observing fellow group members.

Forty years on we are much more aware of the importance of mirroring as a developmental and therapeutic factor than we were when Foulkes first made these observations. Although Freud had, himself, made over twenty references to mirrors and mirroring, only a few of these observations referred to this concept. In Beyond the Pleasure principle,[29] Freud described the child's cotton reel game where the child could allow his mother to go away without protesting by compensating himself through his game in which he staged the disappearance and return of the objects within his reach. In a footnote Freud observes that during the long period of solitude that the mother was away the child had found a method of making *himself* disappear. He had discovered his reflection in a full length mirror which did not quite reach to the ground, so that by crouching down he could make his own mirror image "gone". But Freud did not take this observation further as regards child development and it was Lacan who returned to this in his formulation of the mirror phase.[45/30] Shortly before this in 1917 Freud described "an upright wife and worthy mother of the age of 53" who suddenly experienced a delusional jealousy of her husband. In two sessions with the patient Freud discovered that she was, herself, in love with a young man, in fact her own son-in-law. Not being able to accept this "monstrous and impossible" love, the love had to remain unconscious but displacement on to the fantasy of her husband's unfaithfulness acted "as a cooling compress on her burning wound". Her own love had not become conscious to her but its mirror reflection which brought her such an advantage had now become conscious as an obsession and delusion. "No arguments against it could of course have any effect for they were only directed against the mirror image and not against the original which gave the other its strength and which lay hidden in the unconscious."[30] It is such workers as Winnicott, Mahler, Lacan, and Kohut who have each emphasized some important aspects of child development which they term mirroring. Winnicott with his characteristic sense of paradox said that the first mirror of a child is the mother's face. For in the expression of her countenance the child will first see what he means to her and hence obtain his first self experience. When the mother is unable, through her own preoccupation or troubles, to reflect her infant then he sees not himself but her face and later that child may turn to the physical mirror in order to look for the missing mother, Is this what had laid behind Sylvia Plath's preoccupation with mirrors?

Poem "Mirror", 23rd October 1961.[31]

I am silver and exact. I have no preconceptions.
Whatever I see I swallow immediately.
Just as it is, unmisted by love or dislike.
I am not cruel, only truthful –
The eye of a little god, four-cornered.
Most of the time I meditate on the opposite wall.
It is pink, with speckles. I have looked at it so long
I think it is a part of my heart but it flickers.
Faces and darkness separate us over and over.

Now I am a lake. A woman bends over me,
Searching my reaches for what she really is.
Then she turns to those liars, the candles or the moon.
I see her back, and reflect it faithfully.
She rewards me with tears and an agitation of hands.
I am important to her. She comes and goes.
Each morning it is her face that replaces the darkness.
In me she has drowned a young girl, and in me an old woman
Rises toward her day after day, like a terrible fish.

Was Sylvia Plath's suicide a drowning in the mirror? The terrible fish reminds me of the powerful picture of Escher[32] where the fish broods silently beneath the surface of the water. Borges[33] writes that in the legendary days of the Yellow Emperor of Ancient China the world of mirrors and the world of men were not, as they are now, cut off from each other. The two kingdoms, the specular and the human of these two worlds lived in harmony; you could come and go through mirrors. The inhabitants of these two worlds were quite different until one night the mirror people invaded the earth, but though their power was great the magic arts of the Yellow Emperor prevailed. He repulsed the invaders, imprisoned them in their mirrors, and forced on them the task of repeating, as though in a kind of dream, all the actions of men. He stripped them of their power and of their forms and reduced them to mere slavish reflections. Nonetheless, a day will come when the magic spell will be shaken off. The first to awaken will be the fish. Deep in the mirror we will perceive a very faint line and the colour of this line will be like no other colour. Later on other shapes will begin to stir. Little by little they will differ from us; little by little they will not imitate us. They will break through the barriers of glass or metal and this time will not be defeated. Side by side with these mirror creatures the creatures of war will join the battle. This story powerfully reminds us of the dangers that lie hidden in the mirror image when it threatens to retake a life of its own as it did in our earliest years. Or does it represent the internalized object that has not become integrated with the self?

To return to our developmental line of mirroring. Mahler[9/34/35] has pointed out the "mirroring frame of reference" as the stage when mother and infant present each other with innumerable cues, only some of which are selected for response by mother. The infant gradually alters his behaviour in relation to mother's selective response and internalizes this world of the in-between and thus is born the child's individuality as a reflection of his mother's needs. "It is the specific unconscious need of the mother that activates out of the infinite potentialities those in particular that create for each other 'the child' who reflects her own unique and individual needs". Kohut's concept of mirroring is of the child as "the gleam in the mother's eye" when the mother fulfills the child's phase-appropriate needs for admiration and thereby returns to the child the narcissistic cathexis that he has relinquished in his move from primary narcissism to object-related narcissism, that of the self-object. Kohut's baby is born strong not weak and he is born into the psychological matrix of responsive self objects. He is simultaneously inside and outside of self-objects as oxygen is simultaneously inside and outside of him physically. "Being reflected by the self-objects (mirroring), being able to merge with their calmness and power (idealization), sensing a silent presence of their essential alikeness (twinship), the baby is strong, healthy and vigorous".[36]

Lacan's[4/5/30] thesis is a more surprising one, though it has a very long and interesting pre-history going back almost 2000 years to Plotinus, the neoplatonic philosopher. Lacan refers to the physical mirror, as did Freud, and in his observations the child of six months or so greets his mirror image with intense jubilation. Lacan speculates that the infant is captivated by the unified Gestalt of the specular image in which he has a graceful mobility and a unity that the child himself does not possess in reality. Indeed the child's corporeal self representation is all to pieces and could the child represent it to us it would be like a Hieronymous Bosch painting with limbs askew and with monstrous distortions. The lived self is abandoned in favour of the seductive mirror image that is also more clearly differentiated from the image of the mother than the child has heretofore experienced. Now the fateful process of alienation of the ego begins. The child has discovered the world of the imaginary, of images, the imitation of reality. He is born narcissistically, in love with his reflection and must free himself from this illusion to enter the world of self and others. In this world there is no distance between image and reflection for they are fused. Joseph Conrad in the short novel "The Secret Sharer"[37/38/39] describes how the captain of a boat, troubled by uncertainties as to his fitness for his first command, alienated both from himself and from his crew, helps on board a sailor who is himself a fugitive from another boat where he has been held prisoner for the crime of murder. The captain shelters him in his cabin and gives him a sleeping suit of the same pattern as his own above which "the shadowy head like mine" appears "as though I had been faced with my own reflection in the depth of a sombre and immense mirror". "Everything was as before the ship except that now two of her captain's sleeping suits were simultaneously in use, one motionless in the caddy, the other keeping very still in the captain's stateroom." The captain had to cope with the confused sensation of being in two places at once, a form of autoscopy. Finally the two images separate; the stranger swims away to freedom and the captain steers his ship through an immense danger of darkness where there is no light, no mirror. Now he is fully integrated as the captain of his ship, his first command. The story ends thus: "The secret sharer of my cabin and of my thoughts as though he were my second self had lowered himself into the water to take his punishment calm, a free man, a proud swimmer, striking out for a new destiny."

For Lacan the journey from the imaginary to the symbolic must take place else the individual will forever live in the world of the imaginary. The mirror must be broken if he is to confront himself and his own truth. Conrad's captain has met with his dark side, the split off murderous, oedipal self and he accepted and integrated it. Now he can continue his journey in command of himself, overcome the darkness of depression and the storms of inner and outer conflict. He has passed through the developmental crisis and can fully enter into the role and responsibility of adulthood.

A French colleague, Maurice Laxenaire,[40] reports on a mirror transference in a group using Lacan's theory. Two men of the same age, about 45, look so much alike that the other group members even confuse their names and see them as twins. This twinning preciptates a savage attack by the one, Rene, on the other Luc, as representing all the defects he hates in a man, which are to be soft, weak, erratic and indecisive. Rene says to Luc "you have behaved like a little kid with your father, you don't know how to stand up to him like a man, I'd like to punch you in the face". The therapist interpreted that like twins one can live only if the other dies. "You cannot both be strong at the same time." Rene gradually discovers that Luc represents and embodies a part of himself which he does not wish to acknowledge and so is enabled to begin the process of reinternalization and reintegration that he needs to accomplish his own cure.

The way that individual people mirror and reflect aspects of themselves in the analytic group is often easily observed, especially when we are interested in the process. But other mirroring processes are more obscure which can be identified in the light of the developmental process of mirroring. In Kohut's reconstruction of the developmental line of narcissism the child who has not received phase-appropriate mirroring or has been prematurely or traumatically deprived of an idealizing relationship to the parental figures, will remain fixated at the stages either of the grandiose self or of the idealized parental images. These psychic sub-systems then play an active part in the character structure of the individual and his defences and transferences. It should be possible, therefore, to identify some characteristics of these patients and their responses to the mirroring potential of the group. Some pertinent and original observations have recently been made by a group of Italian therapists headed by Ciani and Fiumara.[41] They observed that the patient whose grandiose self is a principal defensive structure for the maintenance of self cohesion and who is therefore dependent on obtaining environmental confirmation through mirroring of the existence of the grandiose self, will in the group direct his attention almost entirely to the therapist and ignore the other members. Only the therapist can have the exalted status of the idealized parent who then can reflect and confirm the defensive grandiosity. This patient will be greatly threatened by the regressive group processes, by the fusional processes that follow on greater boundary fluidity, for such regression threatens the precarious cohesion of the self and such patients may suddenly leave the group as it begins to "sink in" to pre-oedipal regressive states. Such patients may defensively play the role of the monopoliser, disrupter, clown or critic. The demands they make for emphatic and non punitive yet firm responsiveness by the leader and by the other group members are great, but in my experience can be met.

A group of patients with different disturbances in narcissistic development are those where defensive grandiosity, the pathological grandiose self, has not become the dominant defensive structure. These patients are more silent and withdrawn personalities, who are yet more open to necessary group formative regressions and who in the long term mutual mirroring of group processes are able to give up their schizoid or self mirroring defenses. In the Italian series there was one patient who shared with the group his feeling that he had been born as a Siamese twin but that his twin brother had died immediately after birth. Eventually he began to feel that the group itself had been especially made for him and the twin image faded. Thus he emerged from the mirror world of the imaginary to the shared symbolic world of the group, its relationships mediated through language, and began the process of further maturation within the maturing context of the group matrix. One of my own patients, a computer scientist, who said that he saw no-one when he looked into the mirror, had lived in a world of schizoid science fantasies which formed the predominant imagery of all his dreams and fantasies. He gradually came down to earth as he began to be held in the network of the group and began to experience the reciprocal care and interest of his earthly group companions.

Negative mirroring of the group as a whole towards the individual is reflected in scapegoating phenomena which, within the analytic context, it should be possible to hold and to understand.

I have come to recognize two radically different types of mirroring phenomena; one is primitive, confrontational and destructive, indicating a fixation to a dyadic mode of relationship, the other exploratory, negotiable and dialogical, where both persons, or more than two persons, can share the same psychological space, one in which different points of view are accepted and understood. Patients with borderline personalities and those who show severe narcissistic pathology exhibit the former and it also characterizes destructive intimate relationships between parents and children or between marital partners. I shall illustrate the features of these two types of mirroring with clinical material.

An elderly woman who has suffered a severe narcissistic blow through bodily trauma and marital difficulties has maintained a pattern of behaviour in the group of anger, paranoid sensitivity, selfishness and unhelpfulness to others, despite the tolerance and sympathy she has been offered. Eventually another group member directly, impatiently, but with concern for her and for himself, tells her that she seems to be wasting the opportunities offered by the group. He tells her that she seems to have a fixed frame of reference and to see things only from her own point of view, that she never takes an interest in anyone else nor takes the initiative to lean in another direction. She is either at the centre of attention or not involved at all. She replied mockingly that he seemed to want her attention, to which he was able simply to reply that indeed he did.

He said that for him, the group works by people being mirrors to each other and that if she is not holding up a mirror to him then something important is missing in the group. Following this direct challenge and the demand for attention from her she leaned forward, for the first time asked him about his family life and for the rest of the session remained actively interested and involved. Though, of course, this change in her behaviour did not last and had to be worked at many times, a feeling of flow and rhythm now prevailed throughout the rest of the session with a responsiveness, sensitivity and understanding which had been missing throughout the time that she had been dominating the sessions. On another occasion this same person spoke about her relationship to her children, saying that they keep her in check by telling her very directly what they think of her; they are mirrors to her and she knows that whatever they say about her has a grain of truth in it so that even though it is unpleasant she can accept and learn from what they say. She admitted that without her children she has no viewpoint; thus from her children she received a benign reflective form of mirroring through which she can see herself, in contrast to the destructive and hateful narcissistic mirroring in which she only sees herself ageing, approaching death and which she sees reflected in her ageing husband. Behind this is the unemphatic cold, derisive mirroring that her mother exposed her to throughout her childhood. For many sessions the other members of the group dealt actively with their own similarities and differences to her mode of mirroring; another member told her that he had found that in some rather mysterious and wonderful way a form of transformation takes place in the group, that when you are talking you are either talking about yourself or to another person who reflects some aspect of your own self, that your own problems become revealed and that help comes in some very unexpected manner. He likened it to one of the Moebius strips which appear to be endless and in which one side is always turning towards the other.

In another group Mary, a very intelligent but highly disturbed young woman, whose image of herself is that she is like a moth who defends itself against predators, who are after its juicy body, by markings on the wings that look like enormous eyes, displays towards other persons in the group a clear and deadly vision, like that of the Gorgon. She experiences herself as having a very destructive and concentrated beam of light in her perception of others, and she turns her destructive vision towards another older married woman in the group and attacks her as being totally a caricature of a woman, one who has compromised with society, and has sold out to convention. This projection, in which she recognizes nothing of herself in the other person, enables her to enjoy attacking. This selective perception represents a form of externalization and projective identification in which she attempts to manipulate the other person into representing a bad maternal introject. At the same time she idealizes another woman in the group and says that the reason she enjoys coming to the group is because she sees this other person unthawing, that this person represents her better half, a person who has achieved a form of femininity that she can respect, who has control over her impulses and who is not wracked with problems of right or wrong, over what sort of destructive effects that she has on others. This is an idealizing transference with benign mirroring, whereas for the other woman she has a destructive part-object relationship, using her as a mirror that she would wish to destroy. The selectivity in these responses is remarkable; the woman attacked destructively has the same bad type of relationship with her own daughter with whom she cannot empathise and whom she constantly criticises destructively. The idealized woman feels completely annihilated if she is not responded to sympathetically and desperately needs the type of encouragement and responsiveness that Mary shows to her. On another occasion Mary asks a male member of the group "how much do you know about the therapist? For instance, do you know what he likes for breakfast, whether he goes to the opera?" The man admits he doesn't know any of these things and later Mary explains that she asked this because she has a *benign* view of both the patient and of the therapist and that she sees him as having such a negative and distorted view of the therapist, holding up such a distorted mirror, that eventually the therapist will become discouraged. Here Mary put herself into the position of the benignly involved third person in a negative dyadic relationship who sees the need for a third person to help make the relationship between the other two fuller and more realistic. Though she is not able to accept such a mediation for herself, she sees the great need for it for the other two persons involved. This is a striking example of a person who at one moment is the Gorgon, who can turn from her destructive confrontational dyadic relationship, and become the clear reflective mirror for two persons who would otherwise be locked in just such a destructive dyadic relationship. Through this mirroring a new point of view, which encompasses the destructive relationship and raises it to a higher level of mediation and negotiation becomes possible. You will recall that Perseus was told by Athena, the Godess of Wisdom, that he needed a mirror with which to approach the Gorgon and that without it he would be turned into stone. She loaned him a portion of her armour to act as this mirror. Thus the mirror of Perseus symbolizes that higher level of wisdom that enables us to approach and to master a level of psychological conflict that would otherwise destroy the two persons involved.[42/43] I will return to consider this theme in more detail later.

I have written previously[44] about the need for the therapist to act as negotiator between persons who relate on a mutually destructive dyadic level, one of whom is usually a patient with borderline pathology and the other a person who though not fixated at the borderline level can be drawn into such a mutually destructive dyadic relationship. Both cast motes and beams into the other's eyes. They can only see what they fear and hate in themselves in the other. The role of the negotiator, or the mediator as my colleague Dr Gerald Wooster[45] terms it, is to enable each partner in the dyad to admit that what they attack in the other person is also contained within their own self; "what I say about you is true about you, but it is also true about me; when I can recognize the truth in myself that I am denying, I can also begin to acknowledge the truth in you that I am not perceiving, that you are a whole person with other aspects to your personality". Essentially what the therapist and the other group members do in the group context is to raise the relationship from a dyadic to a triadic level.

What are the mechanisms involved in this form of dyadic and destructive mirroring? This is a narrow form of vision, the other person is seen in the light of a part-object relationship only, other aspects of them are not perceived and the identification of that part of oneself that is similar to that being perceived in the other person is denied. Clearly splitting and projective identification[46/47] are involved, but what is missing is the *point of view* that enables negotiation to take place. There is a head on confrontation and the only outcome, without mediation, is destruction by one person of the other. A patient in individual therapy told me that she was very excited because she felt that she was now beginning to acquire "a point of view". This excites her because it is very useful to have a point of view, which can be played with as a child can play with a new toy. She realizes that when she has her own point of view she now no longer has to involve herself in aggressive confrontations. Without a point of view the only thing she can do when she feels attacked by another person's opinion is to oppose and try to destroy them. Now she is able to say "well, that's the way that you see it, it is not the way that I see it and I have my point of view". Now she has a position in psychological space which is her own and which is not vulnerable to attack by another person. The imagery that I offered her was that without her own point of view she seemed to feel like a prisoner who was pinned down by the beam of a searchlight and the only way to escape from this is to destroy the searchlight, the other person's vision. The searchlight represents the externalization of an internal persecutory super-ego, of a very cruel and unrelenting kind that constantly gives rise to an inner commentary on all her actions and the only other solution to this is to try and evacuate her own sense of consciousness. This was also illustrated by a patient in another group who said that now he found himself being able to reflect about himself for periods of up to sixty seconds at a time. He realized that previously he was always forcing things out of his mind because they were too painful to bear and therefore he was always being over-active and occupying his mind with other things.

The move from the dyadic to the triadic level has been described by Abelin[48/49] as a move from a "mirroring one to one and narcissistic level of relationship" to the "early triangulation" situation of the child who begins to have a point of view on himself because he can identify himself with another person in a three person relationship. For the infant this is predominantly the father, who the child sees in a loving relationship with the mother and by seeing him as a loving person to recognize that he himself is also such a person, loving mother. I shall discuss these issues further but propose once more to illustrate the development of the negotiation perspective with further clinical material. In another group the members were working through the problems of perspective and of being able to see the other person's point of view. Charles, a very successful entrepreneur, is highly effective at negotiation when he has only his own point of view to consider. If he knows the other person's point of view he cannot negotiate. "Everything would then take so long" and he would not be able to make advantageous contracts. Charles has a longstanding marital problem, in which he has not been able to see his wife's point of view; it had been pointed out to him already by another member of the group, who also has a marital problem, that Charles and his wife simply seem to mirror each other and therefore they cannot see the other person as all they see is the mirror image. In this same group, Nancy never has a point of view about the other person; all the truth lies inside herself and therefore no negotiation with another person is possible. The other person has no reality and as a person only exists to confirm or to deny her own sense of reality and of identity. Hence she is enormously vulnerable to a lack of sympathetic resonance from the other person and feels annihilated if there is none. The members of this group are working towards a realization that negotiation and perspective are achieved only if we can contain feared and unwanted aspects of the self; if they are projected into another person no negotiation is possible. The capacity of the group matrix to contain and hold these unwanted and frightening aspects of themselves enables them together to create a psychological space in which renewed negotiation, reintegration and psychological growth becomes possible.

The containment of unwanted parts of the self seems to me to represent the resumption of an internalized dialogue between self and other, basically between the child and the mother. When these dialogues have become 'derailed' in Rene Spitz's[50] vivid phrase, splits in the personality develop and the psychological world is fragmented. This is illustrated by a patient in individual therapy, a brilliant scientist who had to give a lecture before 200 students feared that "unruly persons" inside him would not allow him to give it confidently. These unruly persons are behind the surface of the mirror of the mind. In a small seminar he can get into conversation and then does not fear disruption, but in a large group, unless he can find one person to speak to, he is terrified. The audience seem to represent one enormously large person with whom he cannot have dialogue; interpretation about the mother inside him with whom there is no dialogue leads him to speak forcibly about the way in which negotiation with mother was impossible, no way of feeling acceptable to her; he sees mother as having no ability for dialogue with her own self. The bad relationship between mother and child is located in the group situation and the intimate idealizing relationships represent an escape. In the transference he oscillates violently between good and bad relationships to the therapist, but in the course of therapy he begins to be able to hold two images and two perspectives in mind without the one driving out the other, in contrast to how rapidly he used to move from one state of mind to another, one truth replacing another. Now he begins to be able to inhabit a neutral space, one in which the therapist and he can both exist and from which they can both view the characteristics of either of the two other states of mind idealizing or persecutory. "Shared space is a necessary condition for the differentiation of the individual: it is only when we see people together that we can compare them and recognize what is unusual or unique in each. With shared space we develop the capacity for taking a perspective on a common object of perception. In a shared world the individual discovers his identity, his difference from others; at the same time he subjects that world to an individual point of view, presents it as seen by a particular person at a particular point in space and time.[11] These statements have been made by the art historian Denys Haines[51] who traces the development of Greek art to the point where a shared public space and the capacity for perspective is achieved. The history of the development of the Western mind, as illustrated in Greek art, reflects this development of the individual. The public space of the group offers a forum for the development of perspective, for shared points of view on a common situation and for the transformation of dyadic destructive mirroring to triadic and multipersonal shared perspectives.

I would like to end with a passage from a recent section of the journal Group Analysis entitled "Reflections" in which a student from the Institute of Group Analysis recorded a personal viewpoint on her own personal group analytic experience. It was entitled Face to Face.[52] "I suppose if there were any phenomenon of which one could say with some degree of truth "it's all done with mirrors" it would be group analysis. Like all other conjuring tricks, there remains an element of the mysterious about it, however accurately its component parts are identified and tagged; but unlike other forms of magic, the mirrors *are* there – reflecting not only each other, but also themselves, into infinity . . . Group Analysis taught me to make use of mirrors – to find one's self in and through others; not just to retrieve the lost or buried parts of the self but to discover some I didn't even know were there; sometimes to bring together elements that had seemed irreconcilable and make them, even momentarily, into a coherent whole.

What is the end point of group analysis? Perhaps it is at the stage at which one will no longer need the mirrors, since the reflected parts of the selves will have been reassembled into wholes. That is when it will become possible to see each other. I have, while writing this, suddenly had the conviction that that's what St Paul must have been talking about when he wrote "For now we see in a glass darkly; but then face to face; now I know in part; but then shall I know even as I am known." Knowing, and being known, are what group analysis means to me."

I have tried to make some synthesis and integration of the psychoanalytic, the group analytic and other approaches to recognizing and understanding the processes of mirroring and reflection, using the situation of individual and group psychotherapy for source materials. Moving daily between these two vantage points, the individual and the group situation, one is in an advantageous position to make just such observations. In the group we see daily both the recognition and also the denial of aspects of the self reflected in others and those of others in our own self, the recognition that "I am like you, you are like me this aspect of ourselves: I can recognize, re-inspect and respect that part of my personality: together, if you accept my perception, or I yours, we can learn more about ourselves. Conversely, I can deny your claim to be like me: I am different to you in this respect: respecting our differences we can explore how we differ in this aspect of our personality and each of us will learn more about our invisible selves through what has emerged as an identifiable difference."

References

1. Foulkes, S.H. Therapeutic Group Analysis. George Allen & Unwin, 1964, pages 81, 110, 169.
2. Yalom, I.D. The Theory & Practice of Group Psychotherapy, Second Edition, Basic Books, page 352.
3. Kohut, H. The Analysis of the Self. London. Hogarth Press, 1971.
4. Lacan, J. The Mirror Stage as Formative of the Function of the I as Revealed in Psychoanalytic Experience, in Ecrits. London, Tavistock Publications, 1977.
5. Lacan, J. Some Reflections on the Ego. International Journal of Psycho-Analysis, 34, 11-17. 1953.

6. DARWIN, CHARLES. A Biographical Sketch of an Infant. Mind. July 1877. Volume 7.
7. WINNICOTT, D.W. Playing and Reality. Tavistock Publications, London, 1971.
8. LICHTENSTEIN, H. The Dilemma of Human Identity. Narcissism and Primary Identity, Chapter 8. Jason Aronson, 1977.
9. MAHLER, M. On Human Symbiosis and the Vicissitude of Individuation. Journal of the American Psychoanalytic Association, 15. 740-763, 1967.
10. SHENGOLD, L. The Metaphor of the Mirror, Journal of the American Psychoanalytic Association, 22, 97-115, 1974.
11. BURSTEN, B. The Narcissistic Course in the Narcissistic Condition, editor Nelson, M.C. Human Science Press, N.Y., 1977.
12. AMSTERDAM, B., LEVITT, M. Consciousness of Self and Painful Self Consciousness. Psychoanalytic Study of the Child, 1980, Volume 35 page 67.
13. LEWIS, MICHAEL & BROOKS-GUNN, JAN. Social Cognition and the Acquisition of Self, Plenum Press, N.Y., 1979.
14. DESMOND, ADRIAN. The Apes Reflection. Quartet Books, 1980, London.
15. MCCALL, G.J. The Social Looking Glass: The Sociological Perspective on Self Development. In the Self, Editor, Mishel T. Blackwell, Oxford, 1977.
16. MEAD, G.H. Mind, Self, and Society. Chicago, University of Chicago Press, 1934.
17. STISKIN, N. The Looking Glass God. Weatherhill, New York and Tokyo, 1972.
18. ABRAM, M.H. The Mirror and the Lamp, Oxford University Press. 1953. Oxford University Press paperback, 1971.
19. GOLDING, F. The Mirror of Narcissus in the Courtly Love Lyric, Cornell University Press, 1967.
20. RORTY, RICHARD. Philosophy and the Mirror of Nature. Princeton University Press, 1980. Basic Blackwell, Oxford.
21. BACON, FRANCIS. The Advancement of Learning.
22. RANK, OTTO. The Double. A Psychoanalytic Study. Meridian New American Library, 1971.
23. ROHEIM, G. Spiegelzauben, Leipzig, 1919.
24. SANDER, LUIS. New Knowledge about the Infant from Current Research: Implications for Psychoanalysis, Journal of the American Psychoanalytic Association, 1980. 28.1. 18.1
25. SHOTTER, J. In Life Sentences, ed. R. Harré, Wiley, 1976.
26. LEAL, RITA. Why Group Analysis Works in the Evolution of Group Analysis, Editor Pines, M. Routledge & Kegal Paul, 1982.
27. LOEWALD, H. On Internalization. International Journal of Psychoanalysis, 54, 1973.
28. PINES, M. The Contributions of S.H. Foulkes to Group Analytic Psychotherapy in Group Therapy, 1978, eds. Wolberg, L., Aronson, R., Wolberg A. N.Y. Stratton Intercontinental 1978.
29. FREUD, S. Beyond the Pleasure Principle. 1920. Standard Edition, Volume 18, page 15.
30. LAPLANCHE, J., PONTALIS, J.B. The Language of Psychoanalysis, The Mirror Stage, page 250, Hogarth Press, London 1973.
31. PLATH, SYLVIA. Collected Poems, London, Faber & Faber, 1981.
32. ESCHER, M.C. Three Worlds, in the World of M.C. Escher, p. 124, New American Library, H.N. Abrams, N.Y., 1974.
33. BORGES, J.L. The Book of Imaginary Beings, Penguin Books, 1974, pages 67, 68.
34. MAHLER, M.S. PINE, F. BERGMAN, A. The Psychological Birth of the Human Infant. Hutchinson, 1975, page 221.
35. KRAMER, S. The Adolescent Recapitulation of a Childhood Psychosis: In Separation, Individuation. Ed., McDevitt, J.P. and Settlage, C.F. International Universities Press, 1971.
36. KOHUT, M. Reported in The Bipolar Self. Panel Report. Journal of the American Psychoanalytic Association, 29, 1981, p. 157.
37. CONRAD, JOSEPH. 'The Secret Sharer' in 'Twixt Land and Sea', London, Dent.

38. Cox. C.B. Joseph Conrad – The Modern Imagination, J.M. Dent, London, 1974.
39. Rogers. Robert. The Double in Literature. Wayne State University Press, 1970.
40. Laxenaire. M. Group Analytic Psychotherapy according to Foulkes and Psychoanalysis according to Lacan: in the Evolution of Group Analysis, edited by Pines. M. Routledge & Kegan Paul, 1982.
41. Ciani. N., Fiumara. R., Cajorali. M., Zanasi. M. The Diagnosis and Treatment of Narcissistic Disturbances in Group Analysis. Group Analysis, 178-183, 14.3, 1981.
42. Closs. August. Medusa's Mirror. The Cresset Press, London, 1957.
43. Diel. P. Symbolism in Greek Mythology. Boulder & Horton, Shambhaler, 1980.
44. Pines. M. Group Psychotherapy of the Borderline Patient. Group analysis, 1978.
45. Wooster. G. Resistance in Groups as Developmental Difficulty in Triangulation. Paper given at 5th European Symposium of Group Analysis, Rome, 1981. Group Analysis (1983) XV/1. 30-41.
46. Grotstein. J.S. Splitting and Projective Identification. New York, Jason Aronson, 1981.
47. Ogden. T.H. On Projective Identification, International Journal of Psychoanalysis, 60.3.357, 1979.
48. Abelin. E.L. The Role of the Father in the Separation-Individuation Process, in Separation-Individuation. Editors McDevit, J.B., Setledge, C.F., International Universities Press, 1971.
49. Abelin. E.L. Triangulation, the Role of the Father and the Origins of Core, Gender Identity during the Rapprochement Sub-Phase in Rapprochement. Editors, Lax, R.F., Bach, S., Berland, J.A., Jason Aronson, 1980.
50. Spitz. R. The Detailment of Dialogue. Journal of the American Psychoanalytic Association, 964, 12.752-775.
51. Haines. D. Greek Art and the Idea of Freedom. London. Thames & Hudson, 1981.
52. Garland. Caroline. Group Analysis 13/1, April 1980.
53. Merleau Ponty. M. The Child's Relations with Others. Chapter 4 of The Primacy of Perception. Editor, Ebedie, J.M. North West University Press, 1964.
54. Bach. S. Self-Love and Object-Love: Some Problems of Self – and Object Constancy, Differentiation and Integration. Rapprochement, edited by Lax. R.F., Bach. S., Berland. J.A., Jason Aronson, 1980.

INTERPERSONAL MIRRORING PROCESSES

Reflective	Positive — good qualities recognised, accepted Negative — bad qualities recognized and accepted
Non-reflective	Distortive — selective perception (e.g. scapegoat) Destructive — attack on unrecognised aspects of self in other

SEPARATION-INDIVIDUATION & MIRRORING

0–4	Symbiotic phase	Winnicott Mahler	— Mother's face — "Mirroring Frame of Reference"
4–10	Differentiation phase	Lacan Merleau-Ponty	— Physical mirror and specular image — Alienation from self, externality
10–18	Practising phase	Abelin Amsterdam Kohut	— Early triangulation — Painful self consciousness — Grandiose Self
18–36	Rapprochement phase	Kohut Zazzo/Bach	— Grandiose Self — Perspective on Self as Subject/Object

LIST OF CONTRIBUTORS

M.L.J. Abercrombie, B.Sc., Ph.D., Hon.M.Inst.G.A., is a Zoologist by training, who first became interested in group analysis through researching on problems of observing and reasoning in medical education. She has worked on comparative physiology of invertebrates, Wallerian degeneration of rabbit nerves, perceptual and visuomotor disorders in cerebal palsy children, on selection and training of students of medicine and of architecture and improving small group teaching in Universities. At present she is working in the Radiology Department of the Clinical Medical School, Cambridge. She is a Founder Member of the Group Analytic Society (London) and until recently was its president.

F. Arroyave, F.R.C.Psych., M.Inst.G.A., M.S.A.P., qualified at Salamanca University in Spain. Trained in Psychiatry, Group Analysis and Analytic Psychology in the U.K. Consultant to Oxford Regional Alcoholism Unit at The Ley Clinic, Littlemore Hospital, Oxford. Honorary Professor to the University of the Basque Country. Member of the Training Committee of the Institute of Group Analysis. Continuing commitments and publications concerning his special interest in drink problems.

H.L. Behr, M.B., B.Ch., D.P.M., M.R.C.Psych., M.Inst.G.A., trained in psychiatry at the University of Witwatersrand, Johannesburg, South Africa and Maudsley Hospital, London, and in child psychiatry at the University College Hospital and Royal Free Hospital, London. Presently consultant in child psychiatry at the Kilburn Child and Family Centre and Central Middlesex Hospital, London. Teacher at the Institute of Group Analysis, member of the Group Analytic Society (London) and editor of the journal 'Group Analysis'. Teaches and practises group analysis and family therapy, and has written articles on these subjects.

Patrick de Maré, F.R.C.Psych., is of Swedish parentage, but grew up in England. He had Cambridge and St George's Hospital medical training and qualified in 1941. During his War Service in the RAMC he trained with Rickman and Bion. After organizing an Exhaustion Centre in the European campaign, he returned to Northfield Hospital to join Foulkes and Main in the Northfield experiment.

After the war he became a Consultant Psychotherapist to the St George's Hospital and was co-founder with Foulkes of the Group-Analytic Society in 1952. Later he participated in setting up the Institute of Group Analysis and the Group Analytic Practice. He worked with Benaim and Kreeger at

Halliwick Hospital in a short lived therapeutic community.

He was author of 'Perspectives in Group Psychotherapy' (Allen & Unwin, 1972), and he published with Lionel Kreeger 'Introduction to Group Treatments in Psychiatry' (Butterworths, 1974).

In 1975 he started a large group under the auspices of the Institute of Group Analysis and was joined in this venture by Robin Piper in 1976. From these experiences Piper and he have written a book entitled 'Median Group Perspectives' to be published shortly, from which the chapter in this book was extracted.

Elizabeth T. Foulkes, Hon.M.Inst.G.A., is group analyst at St Bernard's Hospital, Southall, London; Inspector, Department and Lehrseminar für Gruppenanalyse. Akademie für Fachkräfte der Rehabilitation, Heidelberg and a member of the Editorial Committee of 'Group Analysis'. She is a founder member of the Group Analytic Society (London).

S.H. Foulkes died in 1976. He studied medicine in Heidelberg, Munich and Frankfurt. He was a member of the Frankfurt Psychoanalytic Institute until he moved to England in 1933. From 1940, he was a driving force in the development of group analytic psychotherapy. As a Major in the Royal Army Medical Corps he introduced group methods at Northfield Military Neurosis Centre. He was a consultant in psychotherapy at the Bethlehem Royal and Maudsley Hospitals in London, a training analyst and teacher in psychoanalysis at the Institute of Psychoanalysis in London, and a Fellow of the Royal College of Psychiatrists. In 1952, he founded the Group-Analytic Society (London) of which he was Honorary President. He was author of numerous books and papers on psychoanalysis and group analysis and first editor of the journal 'Group Analysis'.

T.E. Lear, F.R.C.P.I., D.P.M., F.R.C.Psych., M.Inst.G.A., Consultant Psychiatrist, St Crispin Hospital and Cheyne Walk Clinic (Northampton), Chairman, Midland Course in Groupwork and Family Therapy and member of the Group-Analytic Society (London).

M.V. Mallon, C.Q.S.W., M.Inst.G.A., Principal Assistant (Development) Social Services Department, Northamptonshire. She studied social sciences at Glasgow University and was tutored in Child Care by Clare Winnicott at the London School of Economics. Subsequently, she became a Child Care Officer and later in the Social Services Department an Area Director. She is a tutor in the Midland Groupwork and Family Therapy Course and organises multidisciplinary training at Cheyne Walk Clinic, Northampton. She is a member of the Group-Analytic Society (London).

M. Pines, F.R.C.P., D.P.M., F.R.C.Psych., M.Inst.G.A., Member British Psychoanalytic Society. He is Consultant Psychotherapist to the Tavistock Clinic (London) and was formerly at the Maudsley and St George's Hospitals. Currently, he is President of the International Association of Group Psychotherapy and was President of the Group-Analytic Society (London). He is Tutor at the Institute of Group Analysis and wrote numerous papers on psychoanalysis and group analysis, clarifying pertinent concepts and including original work on the borderline (psychosis) syndrome. He contributed in and edited several books on group analysis.

F. Beaumont Stevenson, B.A., B.D., M.Div., M.Inst.G.A., Chaplain of Psychiatric Sector Oxford Hospitals. Bishop of Oxford's Community Health Chaplain, Tutor in Applied Pastoral Theology, Rippon College, Cuddeson, Oxford, Lecturer in Pastoral Psychology for Oxford Certificate in Theology, Tutor Midland Course in Groupwork and Family Therapy. Member of Joint Research Committee of the Institute of Group Analysis and the Group-Analytic Society (London), Member of the Group-Analytic Society (London) and of the International Association of Group Psychotherapy. He trained at the Episcopal Theological School at Harvard, Cambridge, Massachusetts; was involved with Ministry to the deaf and become Director of Christian Education, St Edward's Church, Columbus, Ohio and later in the Diocese of Zambia and St. John's Seminary, Lusaka.

V.M.B Stride, S.R.N., Cert.Ed., Dip.Ed., Mal.Ad. For twelve years he has been a remedial advisory teacher for the Schools Psychological Service, Wiltshire County Council, England. She combined her interests in nursing and education to specialise in child development. She is a member of the Wessex Psychotherapy Society and an associate member of the Group-Analytic Society (London).

H.G. Tough, M.B., D.P.M., F.R.C.Psych., M.Inst.G.A., Consultant psychiatrist, St Crispin Hospital, Northampton and the Mayfair Day Hospital, Kettering, Northants. Formerly Supervisor Manchester Groupwork Course, Group Conductor, the General Course in Groupwork, London, and in the Midland Course in Groupwork and Family Therapy, Northampton. Member of the Group-Analytic Society (London).

E.V. Welldon, M.D., M.R.C.Psych. She is Consultant Psychotherapist to The Portman Clinic, London and a Fellow of the Menninger School of Psychiatry. She had extensive experience in forensic psychotherapy, in therapeutic communities, prisons, a school for maladjusted children and diagnostic assessment centres. She supervises group therapists at the Portman Clinic. She is a Full Member of the Group Analytic Society and author of papers dealing with the group therapy of sexual and social deviants.